INSTRUCTIONAL TECHNOLOGY:
The Definition and Domains of the Field

INSTRUCTIONAL TECHNOLOGY:

The Definition and Domains of the Field

Barbara B. Seels, University of Pittsburgh
and
Rita C. Richey, Wayne State University

Association for Educational
Communications and Technology
Washington, DC

© 1994 Association for Educational Communications and Technology

Library of Congress Catalog Card Number 74-70546

ISBN 0-89240-072-2

AECT President: Kent Gustafson
AECT Executive Director: Stanley D. Zenor
Designed and typeset by AAH Graphics, Seven Fountains, Virginia

Additional copies of this book may be purchased by writing to the Publication Sales Department, Association for Educational Communications and Technology, 1025 Vermont Ave., N.W., Suite 820, Washington, DC 20005.

Dedicated

to

DONALD P. ELY

who since 1960 has kept concern

for the definition of the field alive

Table of Contents

Chapter 3
The Sources of Influence on Instructional Technology

Chapter 4
The Practice of Instructional Technology

Chapter 5
Implications of the Definition of Instructional
Technology 115

Glossary of Terms 125

Appendices 135

References 155

Author Index 181

Subject Index 184

Acknowledgments

This book was developed under the auspices of the Association for Educational Communications and Technology in collaboration with the Association's Committee on Definition and Terminology. The authors would like to specifically acknowledge these people.

President of AECT
Kent Gustafson

Past-President of AECT
Addie Kinsinger

Executive Director of AECT
Stanley D. Zenor

Chairperson of the Definition and Terminology Committee (1990–1993)
Barbara Seels

Members of the Definition and Terminology Committee (1990–1991)
Donald P. Ely
Alan Januszewski
James Lockard
Ron J. McBeath
Laverne Miller
Michael Molenda

Rita C. Richey
Kathy Saville
Glenda Thurman
Ellen Wagner
R. Kent Wood

Members of the Definition and Terminology Committee (1991–1992)

Mary Barden
Nick Eastmond
Donald P. Ely
W. Brockford Gordon
Susan Heide
Denis Hlynka
Alan Januszewski
James Lockard

Ron J. McBeath
Laverne Miller
Michael Molenda
Fatemeh Olia
Rita C. Richey
Glenda Thurman
Ellen Wagner
R. Kent Wood

Members of the Definition and Terminology Committee (1992–1993)

Mary Barden
Nick Eastmond
Donald P. Ely
Susan Heide
Denis Hlynka
Alan Januszewski

Michael Molenda
Fatemeh Olia
Rita C. Richey
Michael Simonson
R. Kent Wood

Division Liaisons to Committee
Pat Severenson—DSMS
Ron McBeath—INTL
Ellen Wagner—DID
Kurt Miles—DISC
Larry Cepek—DEMM

AECT Board Liaision to Committee
Michael Molenda   Rusty Russell

Participants in the First Writing Meeting in Pittsburgh (July 1991)
Rita C. Richey
Barbara Seels
Ellen Wagner

Participants in the Second Writing Meeting in Pittsburgh (July 1992)

Barbara Good
Susan Heide
Dennis Hylnka

Fatemeh Olia
Rita C. Richey
Barbara Seels

Participants in the Meetings in Detroit (1992–93)

Rita C. Richey

Barbara Seels

Section Contributers

Ann Bedner
John Belland
Louis Berry
Ed Caffarella
Peggy Cole
Nick Eastmond
Donald Ely
Ken Fly
Denis Hlynka

Alan Januszewski
Michael Molenda
Fatemeh Olia
Allison Rossett
Frank Seels
Michael Simonson
Paul Welliver
R. Kent Wood

Manuscript Reviewers

Roberts Braden
Donald Ely
Kent Gustafson

Graphics Production

Alan Rockwell

Members of the AECT Board of Directors (1993–94)

Addie Kinsinger
Kent Gustafson
David Graf
Larry E. Kitchens
Kay Bland
Roberts Braden

William J. Burns
Joaquin Holloway
Lynn Milet
Ron Payne
Rusty Russell
Jim Stonge

Preface

The Association for Educational Communications and Technology has for the past thirty some years engaged in the lonely and high-risk activity of attempting to define Instructional Technology as a theory, a field and a profession. This definition, which describes and outlines the parameters of a profession rooted in research, theory, and practice, is the result of this continuing effort. It is both an update of previous definitions and a new definition. In conjunction with this effort over the years, several glossaries of the field were created.

The authors and the Committee on Definition and Terminology have worked for three years to develop this definition and the resulting document and glossary. The Committee followed an open process to ensure opportunity for input, and many revisions were made as a result of questionnaires, hearings, and peer review.

Official Endorsement

The Board of Directors of the Association for Educational Communications and Technology has endorsed this definition of Instructional Technology as its *official* definition. The Association, however, is committed to a continuous reevaluation of the definition and to revising and republishing it periodically in order to reflect new concepts and a changing field, profession and discipline.

New Conceptual Framework

Seventeen years ago research, theory, and practice in this field had barely developed to the extent necessary to support a profession. Now, however, we are clearly a profession with an extensive knowledge base and strong scholarly activity. Therefore, this new definition proposes domains of scholarship that support practice. This definition takes the point of view that the field is a mature profession. As a mature profession we have a responsibility to provide a firm basis for making decisions and developing research agendas. Thus, this new definition makes clear the need for an emphasis on research and theory to develop the domains of utilization, management, and evaluation.

At the same time this analysis of the domains illustrates how the field has evolved from one of generalists to one of specialists, but specialists within broad areas of specialization. To function effectively specialists need to be able to communicate with other specialists in the field, and they need to understand how they fit into the field as a whole. The role of the association then becomes less one of an umbrella of organizations with similar interests and more one of a community of professionals with complementary interests who need to communicate with each other and support each other. Similarly, there is a need for the association to provide channels for communication with other organizations that can be supportive of the profession.

The Association believes that:

- this is the best conceptual framework available at this time for defining Instructional Technology,

- this conceptual framework can be easily understood and applied by its members, and

- other conceptual frameworks can, with some analysis, be seen to fit within the conceptual framework offered here.

Terminology

Since the 1977 definition, many glossaries in the field have been published. Some of these are oriented towards terminology for the profession in general and others towards the terms used in a special area or with a medium. A partial list of such glossaries is provided in Appendix A.

The glossary of this monograph includes only those definitions necessary to understand the essential characteristics of Instructional Technology and its domains. It is assumed that the reader also will access some of the many good glossaries available if other definitions are needed.

Summary

The Association officially endorses this definition of Instructional Technology which has been developed over three years by the Committee on Definition and Terminology. The Association recognizes that other theoretical frameworks exist and that these are valid, but believes that these are part of the more inclusive theoretical framework of Instructional Technology used in this definition. In making this definition and the document explaining it available, we hope to help other organizations clarify their relationship to the broad field of Instructional Technology. Although the Association offers this definition as its current position, it is committed to a continuous reevaluation of the definition and to revising and publishing it so that it reflects changing concepts and terminology.

A document of this magnitude can only be produced as the result of the dedication and effort of the persons who formed the committee and of its chairperson, Barbara Seels and her collaborator, Rita C. Richey. Without their energies, skill, perseverance, and willingness to risk stating their perceptions in this format we could not have offered this document. Whether or not we agree with the statements presented here, they will provide a benchmark and a point of dialogue for further development of a profession which seeks to provide conditions for effective learning.

Foreword

The last time the Association for Educational Communications and Technology endorsed a formal definition was in 1977. Now, seventeen years later, it is time to re-look and re-think 'what we are about'. A lot has happened since 1977. Changes in theory, technology and application have revolutionized the field.

In 1977 PBS, the Public Broadcasting System, was just barely struggling to its feet. *Instructional Design: Principles and Procedures*, Leslie Briggs' landmark book operationalizing instructional design had just been published (Briggs, 1977). Also in 1977, the Apple II® microcomputer was introduced and spurred the development and use of computer courseware. By 1984 the graphic capabilities of Macintosh computers were revolutionizing the production of instructional materials. Communications satellites, fiber optics and user-friendly computer languages were not prevalent. Consequently, teleconferencing, interactive video, integrated media, electronic networking and new approaches to the design of courseware had not affected the field because the interactive possibilities of high technology were yet to come.

In 1969 the British Open University experiment changed correspondence education into what we now call distance learning, but in 1977 this new process was still relatively unsophisticated. Since then, great changes have been wrought by the development of telecommunications technology. As a result, distance education can be found as a standard dimension of both universities and schools, providing intra- and inter-organizational communication and connections with remote, rural areas by satellite, microwave transmission, cable and computers.

Other technological innovations had comparable effects. Audio technology has undergone a major transformation as evidenced in the shift from the long-play vinyl record to the compact disc. Motion picture film was largely supplanted by videotape which is currently being supplanted by digitized audio and video. In 1977 teachers had to contend with scheduling and showing film, including threading a 16mm projector so that the upper and lower loops provided just the right synchronization between audio and video. Today, most homes own their own video cassette recorder (VCR) and showing a film is as simple as putting the cassette tape into the VCR. Instructional resources available outside the home have multiplied dramatically. Even in the eighties, the price to purchase or rent an entertainment or educational film was high. Today, every city has dozens of corner video shops, and grocery stores offer video rentals for less than a dollar each. Laser discs are available for home use. Public libraries not only offer videos, but discs and computer software are beginning to be available there as well. Currently, the term "information superhighway" is common vocabulary and use of the Internet is mushrooming.

In 1977 Instructional Technology was an emerging field of study. Although practice flourished, theory was limited. Proliferation of instructional design models came in the 1970's and 1980's. Many models were introduced including Dick and Carey's design model (1978) and Keller's motivation model (1983). The cognitive perspective had not yet come to supersede behaviorism in instructional psychology, and performance technology had not yet become a key concept. The concepts of constructivism and post-modernism were not being discussed.

In sum, much has happened since the last definition of the field. Instructional Technology has evolved both as a profession and an area of academic study. The purpose of this book is to propose a new definition of the field based not only on a reexamination of the 1977 definition, but also upon the developments in research, theory, and practice.

Barbara B. Seels   Rita C. Richey
Pittsburgh, Pennsylvania   Detroit, Michigan

Chapter 1

The 1994 Definition of the Field

Instructional Technology is the theory and practice
of design, development, utilization, management and
evaluation of processes and resources for learning.

For at least forty years the field of Instructional Technology periodically has pursued processes of collective self-examination, resulting in statements which describe itself professionally. In 1963 such efforts produced the first formal definition of the field. This definition has been updated a number of times, with each change providing new directions for the field. Since the last formal definition seventeen years ago, dramatic changes in the profession and in technology have occurred. Consequently, this process of reexamination has once again evolved. The result of this collective analysis is the 1994 definition of the field shown above. This book will explore the dimensions of the new definition and its implications for both theory and practice. First, Chapter One will introduce the new definition by discussing the assumptions on which it was based and the implications of its terminology.

Assumptions of the Definition

The Nature of the Definition

Israel Scheffler (1960) distinguishes between general definitions and scientific definitions. According to Scheffler, scientific definitions are

1

technical, theoretically based and require special knowledge in order to understand them. They are embedded in a context of research. General definitions, on the other hand, can be understood by the public or other professionals. A general definition explains how a term is to be understood in the context in which it is used. Scheffler identifies three types of general definitions: stipulative, descriptive and programmatic. The definition of the field presented here meets Scheffler's criteria for a general definition of a stipulative and programmatic nature. This 1994 definition of the field is based on prior usage, stipulating what the field is equivalent to and encompasses, and suggests areas where research is needed. Therefore, it is a stipulative definition with programmatic implications intended to serve communication purposes.

A field can be defined in several ways: by the roles practitioners play, by areas of special knowledge, or by the requirements for being a professional in the field (Marriner-Tomey, 1989). Definitions can be logical or metaphorical or a combination of both. For example, a role in a field can be described through metaphor, such as portraying the instructional designer as an artist or a craftsman.

Before a definition is developed, parameters for the definition must be clarified. These parameters are the assumptions that provide a basis for making decisions. For a definition to be formulated, decisions must be made first about the scope, purpose, viewpoint, audience and essential characteristics to be taken into account. The 1994 definition of the field is based on the following assumptions:

- Instructional technology has evolved from a movement to a field and profession. Since a profession is concerned with a knowledge base, the 1994 definition must identify and emphasize Instructional Technology as a field of *study* as well as practice. In contrast, the 1977 definition placed more emphasis on practitioner roles.

- A revised definition of the field should encompass those areas of concern to practitioners and scholars. These areas are the domains of the field.

- *Both* process and product are of vital importance to the field and need to be reflected in the definition.

- Subtleties not clearly understood or recognized by the typical Instructional Technology professional should be removed from the definition and its more extended explanation.

Although not stated explicitly, several important characteristics of the field are implicit in the definition. First, it is assumed that both research and practice in the field are carried out in conformity with the ethical norms of the profession. It is further assumed that professional decisions of instructional technologists are guided by their understanding of those interventions which are more likely to yield effective results. Being aware of the knowledge base of 'what works' in diverse circumstances and using that knowledge base are important hallmarks of the Instructional Technology professional. Professional instructional technologists who fail to follow effective practices betray their lack of understanding of or commitment to the norms of the field.

Closely related to the concept of effectiveness is efficiency. The definition also assumes that practice in this field is characterized by efficient, economical pursuit of ends. Another hallmark that differentiates the professional from the lay person is the ability to achieve effective, productive ends in a way that is most direct, adroit, and cost-beneficial. There are many activities conducted by professional instructional technologists that are also conducted by others, such as developing computer courseware, selecting materials to use with learners, or making video recordings. The difference, it is assumed, is that the professional will be able to conduct these activities with a more efficient use of human and material resources. These characteristics and the values they imply are discussed further in Chapter Three.

Educational/Instructional Technology

Historically, the field has been called both 'Educational Technology' and 'Instructional Technology'. Those who prefer 'Instructional Technology' make two points. Their first point is that the word 'instructional' is more appropriate for describing the function of technology. Secondly, they argue that 'instructional' is more appropriate because 'Educational Technology' commonly implies a school or educational setting. To many the term 'instructional' incorporates not only K–12 settings, but training situations as well. Knirk and Gustafson (1986) assert that 'instructional' relates primarily to teaching and learning problems, while 'educational' is too broad, encompassing all aspects of education.

Those who prefer the use of 'Educational Technology' argue that since instruction is considered by many as a *part* of education the term helps maintain a broader focus for the field (Association for Educational Communications and Technology, 1977; Saettler, 1990). They believe that 'educational' refers to learning in many environments, including home, school, work, and that the term 'instructional' connotes only school environments.

It seems that both groups have used the same rationale to justify use of different terms. There are also those who have used the terms interchangeably for many years as noted by Finn in 1965, nearly thirty years ago. The term 'Educational Technology' is preferred in England and Canada; however, the term 'Instructional Technology' is now widely used in the United States.

In the 1977 Association for Educational Communications and Technology (AECT) definition a distinction is also made between 'Educational' and 'Instructional Technology' and 'technology *in* education' based on the scope of each term. In 1977 'Educational Technology' was used to describe a subset of *education* which was involved in solving problems related to all aspects of human learning through complex, interrelated processes. This interpretation allowed 'Educational Technology' to encompass learning through mass media and support systems for instruction including management systems. 'Technology *in* education' was used to describe technological applications used by support systems for education such as grade reporting, scheduling and finance. 'Instructional Technology' was defined as a subset of 'Educational Technology' using the rationale that instruction is a subset of education which deals only with learning that is *purposive and controlled* (AECT, 1977).

Since 1977 the distinctions between these terms have disappeared. Currently, all three terms are used to describe applications of technological processes and tools which can be used to solve problems of instruction and learning. Today the profession is centering activities and concepts around instruction more and more, even if the instruction is incidental (indirect) rather than intentional (constructed or directed). In other words, there is less emphasis on problems involved with all aspects of education and more emphasis on problems related to the effect of incidental or intentional instruction on learning. Therefore, it is difficult to sustain the proposition that 'Instructional Technology' and 'technology in education' are subsets of 'Educational Technology'.

At present the terms 'Educational Technology' and 'Instructional Technology' are used interchangeably by most professionals in the field. Because the term 'Instructional Technology' (a) is more commonly used today in the United States, (b) encompasses many practice settings, (c) describes more precisely the function of technology in education, and (d) allows for an emphasis on both instruction and learning in the same definitional sentence, the term 'Instructional Technology' is used in the 1994 definition, but the two terms are considered synonymous.

The Orientation of the Definition

When the Instructional Technology movement was in its infancy in the 1950s and the 1960s, many of the tools and theories of today were inconceivable. Programmed instruction developers foresaw computer-assisted instruction, but not interactive video or interactive multimedia. Audiovisual specialists saw the potential of games and simulations, but not of video games. The steps in instructional design were simpler then. One had only to master a few techniques and a fundamentally linear theory. The body of research was small because the mass of research on visual learning and other areas was still to come.

Since then society, education and Instructional Technology have become more diverse. The post-1960s period has been one of great technological creativity. Joel Mokyr, an economist from Northwestern University, believes that diversity is the key to continuing technological creativity in a culture (Mokyr, 1990). Diversity, not necessity, is the mother of invention according to Mokyr. Arnold Toynbee, the British historian, argues that when a more dynamic, creative civilization comes into conflict or contact with a more static, less creative civilization, the dynamic civilization will dominate. The society that loses its ability to change and create is superseded (Toynbee, 1957). Similarly, the field that becomes static and uncreative is likely to become less prominent. A definition that clarifies the diversity of interests in the field will identify problems and areas of opportunity that can act as a catalyst for creativity and invention. We now turn to two questions: "What is technology?" and "How essential are the concepts of 'science' and 'systematic' to the meaning of technology?"

The Relationship Between Science and Technology. In his most recent history of Instructional Technology, Saettler (1990) speaks of technology as focusing on improvement of skills and organization of work rather than on tools and machinery. Modern technology is described as systematized practical knowledge which improves productivity. Similarly, Heinich, Molenda and Russell (1993) define Instructional Technology as "the application of our scientific knowledge about human learning to the practical tasks of teaching and learning."

Instructional Technology is often defined as the application of principles of science in order to solve learning problems, a point of view based upon the assumption that science and technology are inseparable. This has proved to be a myth. Science and technology are related, but separable. When considering everyday life in the 15th to 18th centuries, French historian Ferdinand Braudel says that:

> In a way everything is technology: not only man's most strenuous endeavors but also his patient and monotonous efforts to make a mark on the external world; not only the rapid changes we are a little too ready to label revolutions . . . but also the slow improvements in processes and tools, and those innumerable actions which may have no immediate innovating significance but which are the fruit of accumulated knowledge . . . "What I call technology", Marcel Mauss used to say, "is a traditional action made effective". In other words one which implies the action of one man or generation upon another . . . there are times when technology represents the possible, which for various reasons—economic, social or psychological—men are not yet capable of achieving or fully utilizing; and other times when it is the *ceiling* which materially and technologically blocks their efforts. In the latter case, when one day the ceiling can resist the pressure no longer, the technological breakthrough becomes a point of departure for rapid acceleration. However, the force that over-

comes the obstacle is never a simple *internal* development of the technology or science (Braudel, 1979, pp. 334, 335).

Braudel reminds us that technology is not just the application of science, but that it includes improvements in processes and tools that allow one generation to build on the knowledge of a previous generation.

In keeping with Braudel's point of view, the idea that scientists make discoveries and technologists apply them is no longer in vogue among historians (Schwartz, 1992). Things are now thought to be more complicated than that, and technology is believed to stem from other sources in addition to science, such as art and social innovation (Brooks, 1980; Roller, 1971). Therefore, the 1994 definition does not include the concept of technology as *only* the application of science since this is not totally supported by current literature.

The Concept of Systematic. The concept of 'systematic' is implicit in the definition of technology proposed by Everett Rogers. Rogers says that technology is "a design for instrumental action that reduces the uncertainty in the cause-effect relationships involved in achieving a desired outcome" (Rogers, 1983, p. 12). He goes on to say that technology usually has two components: a hardware aspect, consisting of tools, and a software aspect, consisting of information.

Cass Gentry (1991) reviews several definitions of Instructional Technology that do not include 'systematic' as an essential characteristic:

> the body of knowledge resulting from the application of the science of teaching and learning to the real world of the classroom, together with the tools and methodologies developed to assist in these applications (Dieuzeide, as cited in Gentry, 1991, p. 4).

> is concerned with the overall methodology and set of techniques employed in the application of instructional principles (Cleary, et. al. as cited in Gentry, 1991, p. 4).

> an effort with or without machines, available or utilized, to manipulate the environment of individuals in the hope of generating a change in behavior or other learning outcome (Knezevich and Eye, as cited in Gentry, 1991, p. 5).

Still, based on other definitions reviewed, Gentry defines Instructional

Technology as "the systemic and systematic application of strategies and techniques derived from behavioral and physical science concepts and other knowledge to the solution of instructional problems." By 'systemic' he means that all things impact and are affected by other things in their environment. In comparison he defines educational technology as "the combination of instructional, learning, developmental, managerial, and other technologies as applied to the solution of educational problems" (Gentry, 1991, p. 7–8).

The concept of systematic is implicit in this 1994 definition because the domains are equivalent to the steps in a systematic process for developing instruction. Nevertheless, the 1994 definition de-emphasizes systematic in the sense of a linear process that is the totality of the technological approach.

One of the most comprehensive systems-oriented definitions of Instructional Technology was given by Robert Gagné who said that Instructional Technology is concerned with studying and establishing conditions for effective learning.

> Some of these conditions were, to be sure, the capacities and qualities of the *individual human learner*, including such things as visual and auditory abilities, speech and print comprehension abilities, and so on. Other conditions, in fact the other large set, were *media-based* conditions, pertaining to the kind of presentation made to the learner, and to its timing, sequence and organization (Gagné, 1990, p. 3).

Even though this definition is focused on the research questions pursued by the profession, it seems limited now in light of the current constructivist descriptions of learning environments. However, if one assumes that establishing conditions for learning includes establishing learning environments, Gagné's definition still remains a comprehensive, yet precise statement of the concerns of Instructional Technology.

The Structure of the Definition. The 1994 definition recognizes both the established traditions and trends in the field. In the 1970s terminology of the field was rooted in different types of media, including computer-assisted instruction and instructional television, and in teaching activities, such as independent study and simulations. In contrast, the field's current literature contains not only media descriptors, but also learning variables and strategies with more emphasis on techniques and theories than on media categories. In addition, the areas identified by terminology are covered in more depth today. The diversity of the field and profession is reflected in its current terminology and the range of Instructional Technology doctoral dissertation topics (Caffarella and Sachs, 1988; Caffarella, 1991). The 1994 definition provides for current diversity and specialization while incorporating the traditional components of definitions and domains in the field.

The revised definition is:

> *Instructional Technology is the theory and practice of design, development, utilization, management and evaluation of processes and resources for learning.*

Each domain in the field contributes to the theory and practice which is the basis for the profession. The domains are independent, though related. There is *no linear relationship* between the domains. Figure 1.1, The Definition of Instructional Technology, highlights the relationship of domains of the field to theory and practice.

Components of the Definition

According to the 1994 definition, Instructional Technology is:

- the theory and practice;
- of design, development, utilization, management and evaluation;
- of processes and resources; and
- for learning.

The definition's meaning is derived from each component. This section explains the components and how they describe what professionals in this field do and study.

The Theory and Practice

A profession must have a knowledge base that supports practice. Each domain of Instructional Technology includes a body of knowledge

Figure 1.1
The Definition of Instructional Technology

Instructional Technology is the theory and practice of design, development, utilization, management and evaluation of processes and resources for learning.

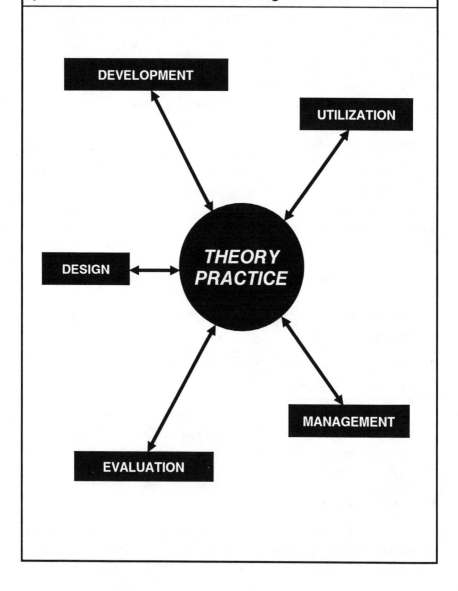

based on both research and experience. The relationship between theory and practice is nurtured by a mature field. *Theory consists of the concepts, constructs, principles, and propositions that contribute to the body of knowledge. Practice is the application of that knowledge to solve problems.* Practice can also contribute to the knowledge base through information gained from experience.

Both theory and practice in Instructional Technology make extensive use of models. Procedural models, which describe how to perform a task, help to connect theory and practice. Theory can also generate models that visualize relationships; these models are called conceptual models (Richey, 1986).

Of the Design, Development, Utilization, Management and Evaluation

These terms refer to both areas of the knowledge base and to functions performed by professionals in the field. These are the five basic domains of Instructional Technology. Each of these functions has sufficient uniqueness and scope to have evolved as a separate area of study. The domain of design represents the largest theoretical contribution of Instructional Technology to the larger field of education. The domain of development is also mature and represents the largest contribution to practice. The domain of utilization, on the other hand, is not well developed either theoretically or practically. Although much has been done in the area of media utilization, other areas of the domain languish for lack of attention. The domain of management has always been part of the field because the resources to support each function must be organized and supervised (managed). The domain of evaluation still rests on research from other fields. The major contribution from this area of study is formative evaluation. The domains of Instructional Technology will be discussed in Chapter Two.

Of Processes and Resources

This phrase encompasses the traditional elements of both process and product in the definition. *A process is a series of operations or activities directed towards a particular result.* In Instructional Technology there are both design and delivery processes. A process implies a sequence involving input, actions and output. The more recent research into instructional strategies and their relationship to types of learning and media is an example of the study of processes (Leshin, Pollock and Reigeluth, 1992). Instructional strategies are methods for selecting and sequencing activities. Examples of processes are delivery systems, such as teleconferencing; types of instruction, such as independent study; models for teaching, such as the inductive approach; and models for the development of instruction, such as instructional systems design. A process is usually procedural, but not always. When a formal set of steps is followed, the process is procedural, but when the order of actions is less structured, the process may not be procedural.

Resources are sources of support for learning, including support systems and instructional materials and environments. The field grew from an interest in the use of instructional materials and communications processes, but resources are not only the devices and materials used in the process of learning and teaching, but also people, budget, and facilities. Resources can include whatever is available to help individuals learn and perform competently.

For Learning

The purpose of Instructional Technology is to affect and effect learning. The phrase was chosen to emphasize learning outcomes and clarify that learning is the goal and that instruction is a means to learning. Learning, as evidenced by a change in knowledge, skills or attitudes, is the criterion for instruction. In the definition, *learning refers to "the relatively permanent change in a person's knowledge or behavior due to experience"* (Mayer, 1982, p. 1040). Berlo (1960) compares learning to the communication process by showing that the ingredients in learning parallel the ingredients in communication. Thus, in communication a message moves through a channel to a decoder who receives it and encodes a new message that provides feedback to the sender. While engaged in the learning process, one perceives, interprets and responds to a stimulus and learns from the consequences of the response.

Evolutionary Nature of the Definition

The 1994 definition evolved from previous definitions of the field. This section will explain how the definition evolved.

Historical Background

Saettler (1990) admits having difficulty identifying the source of the term 'educational technology'.

> It is unclear who first used the term *educational technology*. We have documented evidence that Franklin Bobbitt and W.W. Charters used *educational engineering* in the 1920's. This author first heard *educational technology* used by W. W. Charters in an interview with this author in 1948 . . . The late James D. Finn used *instructional technology* in a forward he wrote for the first publication of the NEA-sponsored Technological Development Project in 1963. However, the focus of the application was *audiovisual communications* (Saettler, 1990, p. 17).

Educators like John Dewey (1916), William Heard Kilpatrick (1925) and W.W. Charters (1945) laid the foundation for the concept of educational technology. But modern technology is primarily a post World War II idea. While the process definition of Instructional Technology has its roots in the educational practice of the progressive era, the popular belief is that Instructional Technology evolved from the audiovisual communications movement (Saettler, 1990). Educational technology was first seen as a tool technology. It referred to the use of devices, media and hardware for educational purposes. Thus, the term was synonymous with the phrase 'teaching with audio-visual aids' (Rountree, 1979).

The field is a result of the flowing together of three streams of interest: media in education, psychology of instruction and systematic approaches to education (Seels, 1989). Two individuals, Edgar Dale and James Finn, are credited with making major contributions to the development of modern Instructional Technology and its earliest definition. Dale developed the Cone of Experience which is shown in Figure 1.2. The cone served as a visual analogy for levels of concreteness and abstractness of teaching methods and instructional materials. The purpose

Figure 1.2
Dale's Cone of Experience

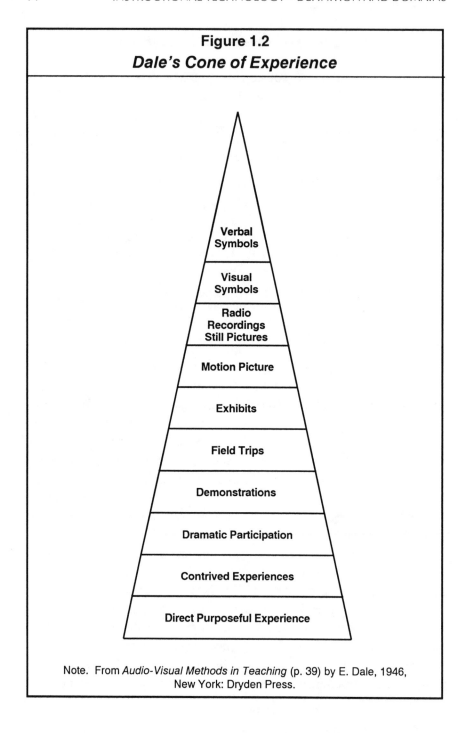

Note. From *Audio-Visual Methods in Teaching* (p. 39) by E. Dale, 1946, New York: Dryden Press.

of the cone was to represent a range of experience from direct experience to symbolic communication. It was based on a concrete to abstract continuum.

It was Dale's belief that abstract symbols and ideas could be more easily understood and retained by the learner if they were built on concrete experience. Dale's cone melded the educational theory of John Dewey and ideas in vogue in psychology at the time. The Cone of Experience was the first attempt to build a rationale that involved both learning theory and audiovisual communications (Dale, 1946).

Jim Finn was a doctoral student of Edgar Dale. Finn has been credited with moving the field of audiovisual communications to instructional technology (AECT, 1977). A major thrust of Finn's work was to change the role of audiovisual communications personnel functionally supportive of the instructional process to one of leadership and innovation. Finn asserted that for audiovisual communications to become a profession the field must develop its own theory, research and technique (Finn, 1953). He argued that Instructional Technology is an intellectual process that must be based on research (Finn, 1960). Finn made two other contributions to the field. He was a strong advocate for changing the name of the field to Instructional Technology (Finn, 1965), and he promoted the application of systems theory as a basis for the field (Finn, 1956). Finn's concept of integrated systems and processes incorporated and expanded Dale's idea of the inter-relatedness of materials and processes.

Definitions of Instructional Technology

AECT's 1963 Definition. There have been many definitions of educational technology (AECT, 1977; Ely, 1983). Six of the definitions are considered mainstays because they are cited most frequently in the literature (Ely, 1973; Ely, 1983). The Technological Development Project of the National Education Association provided the first definition.

> Audiovisual communications is that branch of educational theory and practice primarily concerned with the design and use of messages which control the learning process. It undertakes: (a) the study of the unique and relative strengths and weaknesses of both pictorial and nonrepresentational messages which may be employed in the

learning process for any purpose; and (b) the structuring and system-atizing of messages by men and instruments in an educational envi-ronment. These undertakings include the planning, production, selec-tion, management, and utilization of both components and entire instructional systems. Its practical goal is the efficient utilization of every method and medium of communication which can contribute to the development of the learner's full potential (Ely, 1963, pp. 18–19).

The purpose of the 1963 definition was "to provide a working def-inition for the field of instructional technology which will serve as a frame-work for future developments and lead to an improvement of instruction" (Ely, 1963, p. 8). The definition was one stimulus for changing the name of the organization from Department of Audiovisual Instruction to the Association for Educational Communications and Technology. In the report on the proposed definition the Task Force on Definition and Ter-minology stated, "The *audiovisual communications* label is used at this time as an expedient. Another designation may evolve, and if it does, then it should be substituted" (Ely, 1963, pp. 18–19). Ely believed that there was value in keeping the general term of "audiovisual communica-tions" until personnel in the field were uncomfortable with it (Ely, D. P. Personal Communication, October, 1963).

Another important factor in the 1963 definition was the listing of the roles or functions of those involved with the field. This approach helped move the field from a product orientation, which focused on things and identified the field with machines, to a process orientation, which dictated a dynamic and continuous relationship between events (Ely, 1963).

Finally, there is the mention of efficient utilization. Efficiency is one of the key characteristics of any technology, including instructional technology (Heinich, 1984). In educational circles efficiency can be a "loaded" word because it generates an emotional response. Perhaps this is the reason that the word efficiency does not appear in any of the other major definitions of educational technology. Another acknowledged dif-ficulty with this definition was the decision to use the word 'control'. It was deliberately chosen to suggest that outcomes were highly predictable (Ely, 1973).

Commission on Instructional Technology's 1970 Definition. The second major effort to define the field was made by the President's Commission on Instructional Technology. The commission's report stated that the field could be defined in two ways:

> In its more familiar sense it means that media born of the communications revolution which can be used for instructional purposes alongside of the teacher, textbook and blackboard . . . the pieces that make up instructional technology: television, films, overhead projectors, computers and other items of 'hardware' and 'software' . . . [and]

> [Instructional technology] . . . is a systematic way of designing, carrying out, and evaluating the total process of learning and teaching in terms of specific objectives, based on research in human learning and communication and employing a combination of human and non-human resources to bring about more effective instruction (Commission on Instructional Technology, 1970, p. 21).

The two definitions perpetuated the ambiguity surrounding educational technology. There were several new aspects to the latter definition. First, there was the idea that Instructional Technology must include specific objectives. This is probably due to the influence of B. F. Skinner (1954) and Robert Mager (1962). Their ideas were adopted widely by practitioners in the field. Second, there was the idea that methods and techniques used to teach specific objectives should be based on research. Third, there was the phrase 'more effective instruction'. Effectiveness is also a key characteristic of technology (Heinich, 1984). Nevertheless, the word 'effectiveness' has not been included in the major definitions of the field. Perhaps the reason for this is because effectiveness is typically assumed once Instructional Technology principles are utilized.

A subtle but important difference between the 1994 definition and the 1963 definition is the shift in vocabulary from 'systems' to 'systematic'. The concept of systems can be complicated; perhaps the use of the word 'systematic' was an attempt to simplify and clarify the process of Instructional Technology.

Silber's 1970 Definition. The third influential definition was provided by Kenneth Silber who later chaired the AECT Committee on Definition and Terminology.

> Instructional Technology is the Development (Research, Design, Production, Evaluation, Support-Supply, Utilization) of Instructional Systems Components (Messages, Men, Materials, Devices, Techniques, Settings) and the Management of that development (Organization, Personnel) in a systematic manner with the goal of solving educational problems (Silber, 1970, p. 21).

This definition differs in three ways from the 1963 definition. The notion of development is different in this definition than it was in the earlier definition. In the first definition 'development' refers to the development of human potential, an idea that is important to the more traditional approach of educational psychology. In Silber's definition 'development' is used as an inclusive term to mean designing, producing, using and evaluating technology for instruction. The 1970 definition assumes, as does the 1963 definition, that Instructional Technology is a man-machine system and that experience is interrelated with materials. The 1970 definition follows previous definitions by identifying roles performed by educational technologists. It differs in that it changes the scope of educational technology by listing additional components of the field (i.e. techniques, settings). The extension of components provided opportunity for new investigations under the name educational technology. Nevertheless, the focus on roles and components gave many the impression that educational technology was oriented more to practice than to theory. The idea of 'problems' is first introduced in Silber's definition and is at the core of the definition. The idea of educational technology as a problem solving activity will be included in subsequent definitions. Finally, Silber's definition does not stand neatly by itself. It is essential to read the article which elaborates on the definition in order to understand it. Subsequent definitions also will depend on similar elaboration.

MacKenzie and Eraut's 1971 Definition. This definition from the United Kingdom is succinct, but it seems too broad to be useful for accurately describing educational technology.

> Educational technology is the systematic study of the means whereby
> educational ends are achieved (as cited in Ely, 1973, p. 52).

Previous definitions included the words 'machine', 'instruments', or 'media'. This definition is the first that does not mention hardware or software. It is a process-based account of the field; although hardware may be inferred as part of the means. While the MacKenzie and Eraut definition does not explicitly address the issue, the use of the word 'study' seems to place more emphasis on the idea that Instructional Technology is an intellectual endeavor than do the two 1970 definitions which do not mention this word. MacKenzie and Eraut expand the concept of 'study' by referring to a study of the means. This extension is a much broader concept than the study of pictorial and non-representational messages. The 'systematic study of the means' also infers that educational technology may be considered an area of inquiry. Note also the use of the term systematic. MacKenzie and Eraut thus suggest educational technology is an academic field or discipline. Although the idea is not present in subsequent definitions; it is reintroduced in this 1994 definition.

AECT's 1972 Definition. This definition was approved by the Association and was an outgrowth of the Committee on Definition and Terminology which was active at that time.

> Educational technology is a field involved in the facilitation of human
> learning through the systematic identification, development, organi-
> zation and utilization of a full range of learning resources and through
> the management of these processes (AECT, 1972, p. 36).

This definition states that educational technology is a systematic process for developing and using instructional resources. These ideas are carried over from the 1963, 1970, and 1971 definitions and are incorporated in the 1994 definition. Many of the same roles identified in previous definitions are repeated in this definition (e.g. development, organization, management and utilization). The 1972 definition attempts to identify educational technology as a field (Ely, 1972). The ideas of 'control' and 'specific objectives' are replaced in this definition by the ideas of 'process' and 'facilitation of human learning' (Ely, 1983). This definition left open the possibility that educational technology could be concerned with ends other than pre-determined ends specified as objectives. The use of the word facilitation in definitions of educational technology began and ended here; although Donald Ely commented that the word 'facilitation' would have been better than 'control' in the 1963 definition (Ely, D.P, Personal Communication, January, 1993).

One characteristic of the 1972 definition was the decision to define audiovisual communications as a field. This action promoted the idea that audiovisual communications is a profession. During the development of this definition an important philosophical debate centered around Robert Heinich's idea that the field was defined by the concept of 'system' and Kenneth Silber's emphasis on the function of individualizing instruction as a defining characteristic.

AECT's 1977 Definition. The complete official definition was sixteen pages in length. This is an abbreviated version.

> Educational technology is a complex, integrated process involving people, procedures, ideas, devices and organization for analyzing problems and devising, implementing, evaluating and managing solutions to those problems involved in all aspects of human learning (AECT, 1977, p. 1).

The 1977 definition attempted to identify educational technology as a theory, a field and a profession. With the exception of AECT's 1963 definition, prior attempts at definition had not emphasized educational technology as a theory. The change in wording from the 'men' in prior definitions to 'people' is also noteworthy. It indicates a greater sensitivity to gender issues by both the committee and the AECT organization.

Conclusions

When one compares the definitions just presented, it becomes clear that several concepts appear in many of the definitions although the context and meaning of the concept may vary. Words like 'systematic', 'resources', and 'processes' occur frequently. Words that are precursors of the domains in the 1994 definition also occur in earlier definitions, including 'design', 'development', 'use' or 'utilization', 'organization' or 'management' and 'evaluation'. On the other hand, words used in earlier definitions have been eliminated from later definitions, words including 'control', 'facilitation', 'procedures', 'man/machine', and 'devices'. Each definition makes a statement of purpose related to goals, means/ends, learning and problem solving. Yet when we look at the definitions chronologically, it is interesting that the 1994 definition is closer to the 1963 and 1971 definitions than to later definitions. This is because the stated goal in both was to effect the learning process. It is also because the 1963 definition was based more on theory and practice than on the functions emphasized in later definitions.

In 1973 Ely discussed the idea that definitions of Educational Technology share three major themes which present the ideas that educational technology is:

- a systematic approach,
- a study of means, and
- a field directed toward some purpose (Ely, 1973).

The 1994 definition interprets means as processes and resources and systematic as the domains of design, development, utilization, management, and evaluation. It reflects the evolution of Instructional Technology from a movement to a field and a profession and the contributions this field has made to theory and practice.

Sources of Information

The following sources are suggested for further study of the topics in this chapter. The complete list of references, including those cited in this chapter, can be found at the end of the book.

Branyan-Broadbent, B. and Wood, R. K. (Eds.). (1993). *Educational media and technology yearbook*. Englewood, CO: Libraries Unlimited.

Ellington, H. and Harris, D. (1986). *Dictionary of instructional technology*. London: Kogan Page.

Eraut, M. (Ed.). (1989). *The international encyclopedia of educational technology*. NY: Pergamon Press.

Unwin, D. and McAleese, R. (Eds.). (1988). *The encyclopaedia of educational media communications and technology* (2nd Ed.). NY: Greenwood Press.

Chapter 2

The Domains of the Field

The 1994 definition is built around five separate areas of concern to instructional technologists: Design, Development, Utilization, Management, and Evaluation. These are the domains of the field. In this chapter there are definitions for each of these domains, the domain subcategories, and related concepts.

The Role of the Domains

The Functions of the Domains

To complete the task of defining a field, a means for identifying and organizing the relationships emerging from theory and practice must be developed. Taxonomies, or classifications, are often used to simplify these relationships (Carrier and Sales, 1987; Knezek, Rachlin and Scannell, 1988; Kozma and Bangert-Downs, 1987). A taxonomy is a classification based on relationships. In the classic *Taxonomy of Educational Objectives: Cognitive Domain*, Benjamin Bloom differentiates between a taxonomy and a simpler classification scheme. According to Bloom, a taxonomy: (1) may not have arbitrary elements, (2) must correspond to some real phenomena represented by the terms, and (3) must be validated through consistency with the theoretical views of the field.

> The major purpose in constructing a taxonomy . . . is to facilitate communication . . . the major task in setting up any kind of taxonomy

is that of selecting appropriate symbols, giving them precise and usable definitions, and securing the consensus of the group which is to use them (Bloom, 1956, p. 10–11).

An up-to-date taxonomic structure is essential to the future develop-ment of Instructional Technology and, in addition, the field needs a common conceptual framework and agreement on terminology. Without this framework it is difficult to make generalizations, or even communicate easily across sub-fields. Common understandings are especially critical since much of the work of instructional technologists is done in teams, and to be effective teams need to agree upon their terminology and conceptual framework.

The rapidity of technological change and modification necessitates the transfer of what is known from one technology to another. Without this 'transferability' the research base must be recreated for each new technology. By identifying taxonomic areas, academics and practitioners can work to resolve research issues, and practitioners can work with theorists to identify where theories are weak in supporting and predicting real world Instructional Technology applications. Without clearly delineated categories and functions, cooperation between academics and practitioners becomes even more difficult due to a variety of definitions of the same term. Consequently, the validation of theory and practice can be impeded.

Fleishman and Quaintance (1984) summarized several potential benefits of developing a taxonomy of human performance:

- to aid in conducting literature reviews;
- to create the capacity to generate new tasks;
- to expose gaps in knowledge by delineating categories and subcategories of knowledge, exposing holes in research, and promoting theoretical discussion or evaluation;
- to assist in theory development by evaluating how successful theory organizes the observational data generated by research within the field of Instructional Technology.

Several of the previous approaches to taxonomies of Instructional Technology have used a functional approach. The 1977 definition of the field (AECT, 1977) proposed that instructional management functions and instructional development functions operated on instructional systems components. Ronald L. Jacobs (1988) also proposed a domain of human performance technology that included both theory and practice and identified the functions practitioners fulfill. In Jacobs' proposed domain there are three functions: management functions, performance systems development functions and human performance systems components which are the conceptual bases for performing the other functions. Each function has a purpose and components. The subcomponents of management are administrative and personnel. The subcomponents of development are the steps in the development process, and the subcomponents of human performance systems are concepts about organization, motivation, behavior, performance and feedback.

The Relationships Among Domains

The relationship among the domains shown in Figure 2.1 is not linear. It becomes easier to understand how the domains are complementary when the research and theory areas in each domain are presented. Figure 2.1, The Domains of Instructional Technology, summarizes the major areas in the knowledge base for each domain.

While researchers can concentrate on one domain, practitioners must often fulfill functions in several or all domains. Although they may focus on one domain or area in the domain, researchers draw on theory and practice from other domains. The relationship between the domains is synergistic. For example, a practitioner working in the development domain uses theory from the design domain, such as instructional systems design theory and message design theory. A practitioner working in the design domain uses theory about media characteristics from the development and utilization domains and theory about problem analysis and measurement from the evaluation domain. The complementary nature of the relationships between domains is shown in Figure 2.2, The Relationship Between the Domains of the Field.

It is clear from Figure 2.2 that each domain contributes to the other domains and to research and theory that is shared by the domains. An example of shared theory is theory about feedback which is used in some way by each of the domains. Feedback can be included in both an instruc-

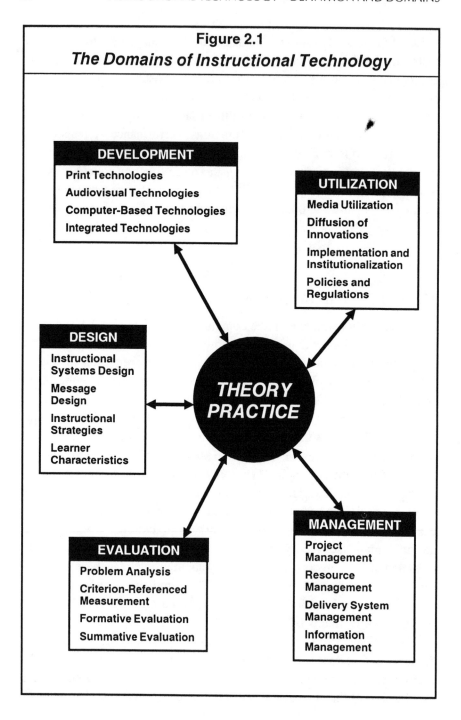

Figure 2.1
The Domains of Instructional Technology

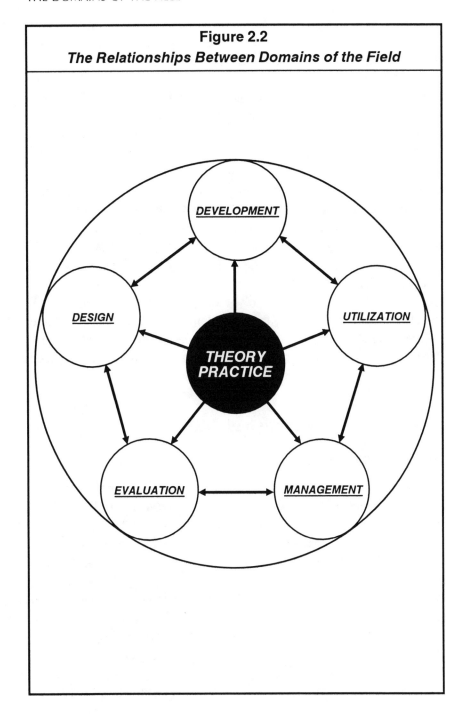

Figure 2.2
The Relationships Between Domains of the Field

tional strategy and a message design. Feedback loops are used in management systems, and evaluation provides feedback.

Although four major subcategories are shown for each domain in Figure 2.1, there may be others that are independent, but not shown. These areas may not appear because the body of theory is insufficient or because they are currently less important. One example is the area of electronic performance support systems which may be given more importance in future definitions and domains of the field. Nevertheless, most areas of the field fit in the subcategories identified. Indeed, some fit in more that one subcategory as is the case with the media selection area which is part of the instructional utilization domain. The pursuit of definitional clarity could lead to specifying the taxonomic levels more completely by breaking each major subcategory into finer distinctions. This task will be left for the future.

The rest of this chapter will be devoted to a discussion of each domain and its relationship to the other domains. For each domain there will be an explanation of its roots, of what it encompasses, of the subcategories in the domain, and of the characteristics associated with each subcategory. Some trends or issues in the domain will be noted.

A Description of the Domains

The Domain of Design

In part, the design domain had its genesis in the psychology of instruction movement. There were several catalysts: 1) the 1954 article by B. F. Skinner on "The Science of Learning and the Art of Teaching" and his theory of programmed instruction; 2) the 1969 book by Herbert Simon on *The Sciences of the Artificial* which discussed the general characteristics of a prescriptive science of design; and 3) the establishment in the early 1960s of centers for the design of instructional materials and programs, such as the Learning Resource and Development Center at the University of Pittsburgh. During the 1960s and 1970s Robert Glaser, director of that center, wrote and spoke about instructional design being the core of educational technology (Glaser, 1976). Many instructional psychology roots of the design domain were nurtured in these Pittsburgh

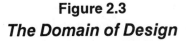

Figure 2.3
The Domain of Design

DESIGN

Instructional
Systems Design

Message
Design

Instructional
Strategies

Learner
Characteristics

associations. Not only was this the home of Simon, Glaser and the Learning Research and Development Center, but Skinner's influential paper "The Science of Learning and the Art of Teaching" was first presented in Pittsburgh prior to its publication later that year (Spencer, 1988).

Complementing the instructional psychology roots was the application of systems theory to instruction. Introduced by Jim Finn and Leonard Silvern, the instructional systems approach gradually developed into a methodology and began to incorporate ideas from instructional psychology. The systems approach led to the instructional systems design movement as exemplified by the instructional development process used in higher education in the 1970s (Gustafson and Bratton, 1984). Interest in message design also grew during the late 1960s and early 1970s. The collaboration of Robert Gagné and Leslie Briggs at the American Institutes for Research in the 1960s (also in Pittsburgh) and at Florida State University in the 1970s brought instructional psychology expertise together with systems design talent. Together they brought the instructional design concept to life (Briggs, 1968; Briggs, 1977; Briggs, Campeau, Gagné, and May, 1967; Gagné, 1965; Gagné, 1989; Gagné and Briggs, 1974).

The domain of instructional design at times has been confused with development, or even with the broader concept of instruction itself. This definition, however, limits design to the planning function, but planning on the micro as well as the macro level. Consequently, the domain's knowledge base is complex and includes an array of procedural models, conceptual models, and theory. Nevertheless, the knowledge base of any field is not static. This is certainly the case with instructional design, in spite of its firm foundation in traditional bodies of knowledge. Moreover, because of the close relationship between instructional design and the other domains of Instructional Technology, the design knowledge base also changes to maintain consistency with development, utilization, management, and evaluation.

Design theory is more fully developed than those facets of the field that have greatly relied upon traditions of practice to shape their knowledge bases. However, with respect to the uses of technology, design research and theory have almost always *followed* practitioner exploration of the intricacies and capabilities of a new piece of hardware or software. This is certainly the case now. The challenge, for both academics and practitioners alike, is to continue to define the knowledge base as well as respond to the pressure of the workplace.

Design is the process of specifying conditions for learning. The purpose of design is to create strategies and products at the macro level, such as programs and curricula, and at the micro level, such as lessons and modules. This definition is in accord with current definitions of design which refer to creating specifications (Ellington and Harris, 1986; Reigeluth, 1983; Richey, 1986). It differs from previous definitions in that the emphasis is on conditions for learning rather than on the components of an instructional system (Wallington, et. al., 1970). Thus, the scope of instructional design is broadened from learning resources or individual components of systems to systemic considerations and environments. Tessmer (1990) has analyzed the factors, questions and tools that are used to design environments.

The domain of design encompasses at least four major areas of theory and practice. These areas are identifiable because they are the categories into which research and theory development efforts fall. The design domain includes the study of instructional systems design, message design, instructional strategies and learner characteristics. Definitions and descriptions for each of these areas follow.

Instructional Systems Design. *Instructional Systems Design (ISD)* *is an organized procedure that includes the steps of analyzing, designing, developing, implementing and evaluating instruction.* The word 'design' has meaning at both the macro- and micro-level in that it refers to both the systems approach and to a step in the systems approach. The steps in the process each have a separate base in theory and practice as does the overall ISD process. In simple terms, analyzing is the process of defining what is to be learned; designing is the process of specifying how it is to be learned; developing is the process of authoring and producing the instructional materials, implementing is actually using the materials and strategies in context, and evaluating is the process of determining the adequacy of the instruction. ISD is generally a linear and iterative procedure which demands thoroughness and consistency. It is characteristic of the process that all of the steps must be completed in order to serve as a check and balance on each other. In ISD, the process is as important as the product because confidence in the product is based on the process.

Message Design. *Message design involves "planning for the manipulation of the physical form of the message"* (Grabowski, 1991, p. 206). It encompasses principles of attention, perception and retention that direct specifications for the physical form of messages which are intended to communicate between a sender and a receiver. Fleming and Levie (1993) limit messages to those patterns of signs or symbols that modify cognitive, affective or psychomotor behavior. Message design deals with the most micro of levels through small units such as individual visuals, sequences, pages and screens. Another characteristic of message design is that designs must be specific to both the medium and the learning task. This means that principles for message design will differ depending on whether the medium is static, dynamic or a combination of both (e.g., a photograph, a film or a computer graphic), and on whether the task involves concept or attitude formation, skill or learning strategy development, or memorization (Fleming, 1987; Fleming and Levie, 1993).

Instructional Strategies. *Instructional strategies are specifications for selecting and sequencing events and activities within a lesson.* Research on instructional strategies has contributed to knowledge about the components of instruction. A designer uses instructional strategy theories or components as principles of instruction. Characteristically, instructional strategies interact with learning situations. These learning situations are often described by models of instruction. The model of instruction and the instructional strategy needed to implement the model differ depending on the learning situation, the nature of the content and the type of learning desired (Joyce and Weil, 1972; Merrill, Tennyson, and Posey, 1992; Reigeluth, 1987a). Instructional strategy theories cover learning situations, such as situated or inductive learning, and components of the teaching/learning process, such as motivation and elaboration (Reigeluth, 1987b).

Reigeluth (1983a) differentiated between macro- and micro-strategies:

> Micro-strategy variables are elemental methods for organizing the instruction on a single idea (i.e. a single concept, principle, etc.). They include such strategy components as definition, example, practice, and alternate representation . . . Macro-strategy variables are elemental methods for organizing those aspects of instruction that relate to *more than one* idea, such as sequencing, synthesizing, and summarizing (previewing and reviewing) the ideas that are taught (p. 19).

Since 1983, the terms have been used more generally to compare the design of a curriculum with the design of a lesson (Smith and Ragan, 1993a). The more typical use of the terms today is for micro-design to be synonymous with instructional strategy design and macro-design to refer to the steps in the ISD process. The phrases "micro-strategy" and "macro-strategy" are not often used today.

Micro-design has also broadened in meaning to provide for specifications for even smaller units of instruction, such a text pages, screens, and visuals. Thus, there are those now who use the term "micro-design", or "micro-level", to refer to message design, as well as to instructional strategy design. Micro-design at the message design level will be discussed in Chapter Three.

Learner Characteristics. *Learner characteristics are those facets of the learner's experiential background that impact the effectiveness of a learning process.* Research on learner characteristics often overlaps research on instructional strategies, but it is done for a different purpose:

to describe facets of the learner that need to be accounted for in design. Research on motivation is an example of an overlapping area. The instructional strategy area uses motivation research to specify the design of components of instruction. The learner characteristics area uses motivation research to identify variables that should be taken into account and to specify how to take them into account. Learner characteristics, therefore, impact the components of instruction studied under instructional strategies. They interact not only with strategies but also with the situation or context and content (Bloom, 1976; Richey, 1992).

Trends and Issues. Trends and issues in the design domain cluster around the use of traditional instructional systems design (ISD) models, the application of learning theory to design, and the impact of the new technologies on the design process. Although there is consensus that the more traditional systematic approach to instructional design is still of major significance, some are raising questions regarding the efficacy of ISD models, and the tendency to use them in an inflexible, linear manner. Dick (1993) advocates an *enhanced* ISD that incorporates elements of the performance technology approach, attempts to reduce the typical ISD cycle time, and places an increased emphasis on electronic performance support systems. There is also a growing concern about the absence of ISD in the schools as a means of curriculum design. Some are calling for a more thorough examination of the applicability of standard ISD procedures for use in schools whether one is planning instruction for children or staff development for teachers and administrators (Gustafson, 1993; Martin and Clemente, 1990; Richey and Sikorski, 1993).

One issue of great importance is the need for theory which relates learning classification to media selection. Each of the steps in the ISD process, from task analysis to evaluation, with the exception of media selection, has a basis in learning classification theory and procedures for implementing that theory. Although some media selection models require consideration of types of learning (Reiser and Gagné, 1982), ways to base these decisions on objectives and strategies while taking other variables into account are insufficiently developed.

With respect to other theoretical issues, there are concerns that practitioners typically emphasize only those general design steps highlighted in an ISD model and ignore the use of general learning principles (Winn, 1989). However, there are also questions as to the most appropriate orientation to learning. The field has been voicing a cognitive stance, even though procedures and tactics reflect both a behavioral and cognitive orientation. Today there is also growing support for the constructivist position, resulting in an emphasis on learner experience, learner control and learner definitions of meaning and reality. This is consistent with the trend towards contextualization of content which is evident in the situated and anchored learning research (Cognition and Technology Group at Vanderbilt, 1992), the performance technology movement and the systemic approach to designing instruction (Richey, 1993a). The search for collaboratively and cooperatively-based alternatives to individualized and independent learning approaches is another example of pressure to develop alternative strategies. Perhaps the more basic trend will be the acceptance of alternative approaches to design.

Regardless of one's philosophical or theoretical orientation, all designers are being affected by the rapid advancements in technology which provide new platforms for instructional delivery, as well as a means of automating facets of the design process itself. As a delivery alternative, these technologies allow not only more effective visualization, but also instant access to information, the ability to link information, more adaptable and interactive design, and learning through other than formal means (Hannafin, 1992). As a means of automating design, the new technologies allow designers to use more detailed rules for instructional strategy selection, implement "just-in-time" training, and efficiently respond to the expectations and requirements of their organizations (Dick, 1993). These trends are a reaction to issues and affect the fundamentals of instructional design (Richey, 1993a; Seels, 1993a;).

The Domain of Development

The roots of the development domain are in the area of media production, and through the years changes in media capabilities have led to changes in the domain. Although the development of textbooks and other instructional aids preceded film, the emergence of film was the first major landmark in the progression from the audio-visual movement to the modern day Instructional Technology era. In the 1930s theatrical film began

---

Figure 2.4
The Domain of Development

DEVELOPMENT
Print Technologies
Audiovisual Technologies
Computer-Based Technologies
Integrated Technologies

---

to be used instructionally. As a result, the first film catalogs appeared; film libraries and companies were established; film studies were undertaken and commercial organizations, such as the Society for Visual Education, were established. These events stimulated not only the production of materials for education, but also journals about these materials, such as *Educational Screen* and *See and Hear*.

During World War II, many types of materials were produced for military training, especially films (Saettler, 1968). After the war, the new medium of television was also applied to education, and a new genre of television program emerged. Concurrently, large scale government funding supported curriculum projects which incorporated other types of instructional media. During the late 1950s and early 1960s programmed instructional materials were developed. By the 1970s computers were used for instruction, and simulation games were in vogue in schools. During the 1980s theory and practice in the area of computer-based instruction came to fruition, and by the 1990s computer-based integrated multimedia was part of the domain.

Development is the process of translating the design specifications into physical form. The development domain encompasses the wide variety of technologies employed in instruction. It is not, however, isolated from the theory and practice related to learning and design. Nor does it function independently of evaluation, management or utilization. Rather, development is driven by theory and design and must respond to the formative demands of evaluation and utilization practices and management needs. Similarly, the development domain does not consist solely of the hardware of instruction but incorporates both hardware and software, visual and auditory materials, as well as the programs or packages which integrate the various parts.

Within the development domain, there exists a complex interrelationship between the technology and the theory which drives both message design and instructional strategies. Basically, the development domain can be described by:

- the message which is content driven;

- the instructional strategy which is theory driven; and

- the physical manifestation of the technology—the hardware, software and instructional materials.

The last of these descriptors, technology, represents the driving force of the development domain. Starting from this assumption, we can define and describe the various types of instructional media and their characteristics. This process should not, however, be thought of as simply a categorization, but instead as an elaboration of the characteristics that technology draws from theory and design principles.

The development domain can be organized into four categories: print technologies (which provide the foundation for the other categories), audiovisual technologies, computer-based technologies, and integrated technologies. Because the development domain encompasses design, production, and delivery functions; a material can be designed using one type of technology, produced using another, and delivered using a third. For example, message design specifications can be translated into script or storyboard form using a computer-based technology; then, the script or storyboard can be produced using audiovisual technologies and delivered using an integrated technology, such as interactive multimedia. Within the development domain, the concept of design assumes a third meaning. In addition to referring to macro-level instructional systems design (identifying goals, content, and objectives) and micro-level instructional design (specifying and sequencing activities), design can also refer to specialized applications, such as screen design in the development domain.

The sub-categories of the development domain reflect chronological changes in technology. As one technology gives way to another there is an overlap between the old and the new. For example, the oldest technologies are print technologies based on mechanical principles. The audiovisual technologies followed as ways to utilize mechanical and electronic inventions within an educational setting. Microprocessor-based technologies led to computer applications and interactivity, and today elements of the print technologies are often combined with computer-based technologies, as in desk top publishing. With the digitized age, it is now possible to integrate the old technological forms, and thus capitalize on the advantages of each.

Print Technologies. *Print technologies are ways to produce or deliver materials, such as books and static visual materials, primarily through mechanical or photographic printing processes.* This subcategory includes text, graphic, and photographic representation and reproduction. Print and visual materials involve the most basic and pervasive technologies. They provide the foundation for both the development and utilization of most other instructional materials. These technologies generate materials in hard copy form. Text displayed by a computer is an example of the use of computer-based technology for production. When that text is printed in hard copy to be used for instruction, it is an example of delivery in a print technology.

The two components of this technology are verbal text materials and visual materials. The development of both types of instructional material relies heavily upon the theory related to visual perception, reading, and human information processing, as well as theories of learning. The oldest and still the most common instructional materials occur in the form of textbooks in which sensory impressions, implied through linguistic mediators and printed visual material, represents reality. The relative effectiveness of different degrees of realism has been addressed by a number of conflicting theories (Dwyer, 1972; 1978). In its purest form, visual media can carry the complete message, but this is generally not the case in most instructional exchanges. Most commonly, a combination of textual and visual information is provided.

The manner in which both print and visual information is organized can contribute greatly to the types of learning which will occur. At the most basic level, simple text books provide sequentially organized, yet randomly accessible information in a "user-friendly" manner. Other forms of print technologies, such as programmed instruction, have been developed based upon other theoretical prescriptions and instructional strategies. Specifically, print/visual technologies have the following characteristics:

- text is read linearly, whereas visuals are scanned spatially;
- both usually provide one-way, receptive communication;
- they present static visuals;
- their development relies strongly on principles of linguistics and visual perception;
- they are learner-centered; and
- the information can be reorganized or restructured by the user.

Audiovisual Technologies. *Audiovisual technologies are ways to produce or deliver materials by using mechanical or electronic machines to present auditory and visual messages.* Audiovisual instruction is most obviously characterized by the use of hardware in the teaching process. Audiovisual machines make possible the projection of motion pictures, the playback of sounds, and the display of large visuals. Audiovisual instruction is defined as the production and utilization of materials that involve learning through sight and hearing and that do not depend exclusively on the comprehension of words or other similar symbols. Typically, audiovisual technologies project material, such as films, slides and transparencies. Television, however, represents a unique technology in that it bridges from audiovisual to computer-based and integrated technologies. Video, when produced and stored as videotape, is clearly audiovisual in nature since it is linear and generally intended for expository presentation rather than interaction. When the video information is on a videodisc, it becomes randomly accessible and demonstrates most of the characteristics of computer-based or integrated technologies, i.e. non-linear, random access and learner driven.

Specifically, audiovisual technologies tend to have the following characteristics:

- they are usually linear in nature;
- they usually present dynamic visuals;
- they typically are used in a manner pre-determined by the designer/developer;
- they tend to be physical representations of real and abstract ideas;
- they are developed according to principles of both behavioral and cognitive psychology; and
- they are often teacher-centered and involve a low degree of learner interactivity.

Computer-based Technologies. *Computer-based technologies are ways to produce or deliver materials using microprocessor-based resources.* Computer-based technologies are distinguished from other technologies because information is stored electronically in the form of digital data rather than as print or visuals. Basically, computer-based technologies use screen displays to present information to students. The various types of computer applications are generally called computer-based instruction (CBI), computer-assisted instruction (CAI), or computer-managed instruction (CMI). These applications were developed almost directly from behavioral theory and programmed instruction, but today reflect a more cognitive theoretical base (Jonassen, 1988). Specifically, the four CBI applications are tutorials, where primary instruction is presented; drill and practice, which helps the learner to develop fluency in previously learned material; games and simulations, which afford opportunities to apply new knowledge; and databases, which enable learners to access large data structures on their own or using externally-prescribed search protocols.

Computer-based technologies, both hardware and software, generally have these characteristics:

- they can be used in random or nonsequential, as well as linear ways;

- they can be used the way the learner desires, as well as in ways the designer/developer planned;
- ideas usually are presented in an abstract fashion with words and symbols and graphics;
- the principles of cognitive science are applied during development; and
- learning can be student-centered and incorporate high learner interactivity.

Integrated Technologies. *Integrated technologies are ways to produce and deliver materials which encompass several forms of media under the control of a computer.* Many believe that the most sophisticated technique for instruction involves the integration of several forms of media under the control of a computer. Examples of the hardware components of an integrated system could include a powerful computer with large amounts of random access memory, a large internal hard drive, and a high resolution color monitor. Peripheral devices controlled by the computer would include videodisc players, additional display devices, networking hardware, and audio systems. Software may include videodiscs, compact discs, networking software, and digitized information. These all may be controlled by a hypermedia lesson running under an authoring system such as HyperCard™ or Toolbook™. A primary feature of this technology is the high degree of learner interactivity among the various information sources.

Integrated technology instruction has the following characteristics:

- it can be used in random or nonsequential, as well as linear ways;
- it can be used the way the learner desires, not only in ways the developer planned;
- ideas are often presented realistically in context of the learner's experiences, according to what is relevant to the learner, and under the control of the learner;
- principles of cognitive science and constructivism are applied in the development and utilization of the lesson;

- learning is cognitively-centered and organized so that knowledge is constructed as the lesson is used;
- materials demonstrate a high degree of learner interactivity; and
- materials integrate words and imagery from many media sources.

Trends and Issues. Trends and issues in the print technologies and audiovisual technologies include increased attention to text design and visual complexity and to the use of color for cueing (Berry, 1992). Trends and issues in the computer-based technologies and integrated technologies areas of the development domain relate to design challenges for interactive technologies, application of constructivist and social learning theory, expert systems and automated development tools, and applications for distance learning.

For example, there is currently great interest in integrated learning systems (ILS) and electronic performance support systems (EPSS). ILS's are "complex, integrated hardware/software management systems using computer-based instruction" (Bailey, 1992, p. 5). These systems are characterized by lessons which are: 1) based on objectives; 2) integrated into the curriculum; 3) delivered through networks; and 4) include performance tracking components (Bailey, 1992).

> Specifically these systems can randomly generate problems, adjust the sequence and difficulty of problems based on student performance, and provide appropriate and immediate feedback (in private). Instruction is 'individualized' and 'personalized' with ILS's (Bailey, 1992, p.5).

Gloria Gery (1991) similarly describes the sophisticated performance support systems used in industry which combine hardware and software components to provide an 'infobase', computer-based management, expert tutoring, and job aids and tools within one system. EPSS is a concept, not a technology.

ILS's and EPSS's are examples of the trend toward greater integration of the development domain with other domains such as design, management, and evaluation. As instructional projects become more sophisticated, the demarcations between domains blur and the activities of one domain are inescapably dependent on the activities of another.

The Domain of Utilization

Utilization may have the longest heritage of any of the domains of Instructional Technology, in that the regular *use* of audiovisual materials predates the widespread concern for the systematic design and production of instructional media. The domain of utilization began with the visual education movement which flourished during the first decade of this century when school museums were established. The first systematic experiments in the preparation of exhibits for instructional purposes were conducted. Also during the early years of the twentieth century, teachers were finding ways to use theatrical films and short subjects in the classroom, thus creating a market for films designed specifically for educational purposes. By 1923 visual education budgets in city school systems covered projectors, stereopticons, film rentals and lantern slides. Among the earliest formal research on educational applications of media was Lashley and Watson's program of studies on the use of World War I military training films (on the prevention of venereal disease) with civilian audiences. The focus was on how these films might be used to best effect. McCluskey and Hoban's research in the 1930s also focused primarily on the classroom effects of different film utilization practices (Saettler, 1968; 1990).

After World War II, the audiovisual instruction movement organized and promoted the use of materials. The available supply of instructional materials expanded as production increased leading to new ways to assist teachers. During the 1960s instructional media centers were established in many schools and colleges, and curriculum projects incorporating media became available. These events all contributed to the utilization domain. Probably the most significant event, however, was the publication in 1946 of the first post World War II textbook devoted to utilization, *Audiovisual Materials in Teaching* (Dale, 1946), which attempted to provide a general rationale for the selection of appropriate learning materials and activities. Published in several languages and used all over the world, new editions of this text appeared regularly for the next 20 years. It led to other textbooks on utilization that were used in a widely taught course introducing teachers to audiovisual materials. In 1982 Heinich, Molenda, and Russell's *Instructional Materials and the*

> ## Figure 2.5
> ### *The Domain of Utilization*
>
> | **UTILIZATION** |
> | --- |
> | **Media Utilization** |
> | **Diffusion of Innovations** |
> | **Implementation and Institutionalization** |
> | **Policies and Regulations** |

New Technologies of Instruction was published. This updated the utilization information presented to pre- and in-service teachers, and became another landmark text on utilization. After several editions, the ASSURE model presented in this text has become a widely disseminated procedural guide to help instructors plan for and implement the use of media in teaching. The steps in this model are: Analyze learners, State objectives, Select media and materials, Utilize media and materials, Require learner participation, Evaluate and revise.

The growth of theory during the 1970s and 1980s produced several texts on media selection. Media selection processes are represented through instructional design models because they are systematic (Reynolds and Anderson, 1991). Media selection is a step in instructional systems design, and when the teacher selects media, he or she is performing an instructional design function, not a utilization function. Media selection is so closely related to utilization that it overlaps the design and utilization domains. When media selection is done by someone who uses a systematic design process, it is a design task. When it is done based on subject content or media characteristics using a simpler design process, it is closer to a utilization task. Thus, here again we see the integrated nature of the taxonomy associated with the 1994 definition of the field.

For many years the utilization domain was centered around the activities of teachers and media specialists who aided teachers. Models and theories in the domain of utilization have tended to focus on the user's perspective. In the late 1960s, however, the concept 'diffusion of innovations', referring to the communication process used to spread information and involve users in order to facilitate adoption of an idea, was introduced and attention turned to the provider's perspective. This area was stimulated by the publication of *Diffusion of Innovations* by Everett M. Rogers in 1962. This book has gone through several editions. Starting with 405 studies culled from fields as diverse as education, medicine, public policy, and farming, the author analyzed and synthesized findings from these fields. The synthesis was reported with a model and case histories to substantiate propositions about the stages, process and variables involved in diffusion, which was defined as the spread, adoption and maintenance of an innovation. More recently, Rogers (1983) expanded the study to over 3000 case histories. The importance of this area for the utilization function is that utilization depends on the promotion of awareness, trial and adoption of innovations. Since the book was first published other scholars have pursued questions related to innovation, contributed to the knowledge base in this area, and developed other innovation and diffusion models.

AECT's 1977 definition linked utilization and dissemination into one function, Utilization-Dissemination. The purpose of the function was "to bring learners into contact with information about educational technology" (AECT, 1977, p. 66). The 1977 definition also included a separate function called utilization which was similarly defined as "bringing learners into contact with learning resources and instructional systems components" (p. 65). In the 1994 definition, dissemination tasks, meaning "deliberately and systematically making others aware of a development by circulating information" (Ellington and Harris, 1986, p. 51), are included in the diffusion of innovations sub-category of the utilization domain.

Once a product has been adopted the processes of implementation and institutionalization begin. In order to evaluate the innovation, implementation must occur. While the instructional design literature considers implementation a required step prior to evaluation, it is not considered necessary for the step to occur before specifications for instruction are determined. Consequently, little design literature addresses the implementation process. Like summative evaluation and diffusion planning, implementation planning is often omitted due to a shortage of time and money.

The research base of implementation and institutionalization is not as well developed as other areas, although contributions have been made from the literature on organizational development and education. *Organizational Development (OD) is defined as "a response to change, a complex educational strategy intended to change the beliefs, attitudes, values, and structure of organizations so that they can better adapt to new technologies, markets, and challenges, and the dizzying rate of change itself"* (Bennis, 1969, p. 2). As such, it promotes planned organizational change (Cunningham, 1982). The difference between diffusion of innovations and organizational development is that OD is primarily concerned with change in organizations, and diffusion of innovations is primarily concerned with individuals accepting and using ideas. The overlap between these two concepts is evident. The literature on organizational development is helpful in understanding implementation and institutionalization.

The concept of institutionalization is prominent in other sectors of education. It refers to the integration of the innovation within the structure of the organization. The process and variables affecting implementation and institutionalization of curricular innovations are described in a ten-year follow-up study of the quarter plan to provide year-round schools in grades 9–12 in Buena Vista, California. Based on this study, the administration, faculty, and students recommended that their board of education institutionalize the four quarter system including a voluntary fourth quarter by providing adequate funds (Bradford, 1987).

Historically, each domain has policies and regulations associated with it. It is the domain of utilization, however, that is most affected by policies and regulations. The use of television programming, for example, is heavily regulated. The copyright law affects the use of print, audiovisual, computer-based and integrated technologies. State policy and regulations affect the use of technology in the curriculum. Thus, the study and practice of institutionalization may lead to involvement in issues of policy formation, political behavior, organizational development, ethics, and sociological or economic principles. Institutionalization may require the adjustment of laws, regulations, or policies either at the local level or higher.

The utilization function is important because it addresses the interface between the learner and the instructional material or system. This is obviously a critical function because use by learners is the only *raison d'être* of instructional materials. Why bother acquiring or creating materials if they are not going to be used? The domain of utilization encompasses a wide range of activities and teaching strategies.

Utilization then requires systematic use, dissemination, diffusion, implementation, and institutionalization. It is constrained by policies and regulations. The utilization function is important because it describes the interface between the learner and instructional materials and systems. The four subcategories in the domain of utilization are: media utilization, diffusion of innovations, implementation and institutionalization, and policies and regulations.

Utilization is the act of using processes and resources for learning. Those engaged in utilization are responsible for matching learners with specific materials and activities, preparing learners for interacting with the selected materials and activities, providing guidance during engagement, providing for assessment of the results, and incorporating this usage into the continuing procedures of the organization.

Media Utilization. *Media utilization is the systematic use of resources for learning.* The media utilization process is a decision-making process based on instructional design specifications. For example, how a film is introduced or "followed-up" should be tailored to the type of learning desired. Principles of utilization also are related to learner characteristics. A learner may need visual or verbal skill assistance in order to profit from an instructional practice or resource.

Diffusion of Innovations. *Diffusion of innovations is the process of communicating through planned strategies for the purpose of gaining adoption.* The ultimate goal is to bring about change. The first stage in the process is to create awareness through dissemination of information. The process includes stages such as awareness, interest, trial and adoption. Rogers (1983) describes the stages as knowledge, persuasion, decision, implementation, and confirmation. Characteristically, the process follows a communications process model which uses a multi-step flow including communication with gatekeepers and opinion leaders.

Implementation and Institutionalization. *Implementation is using instructional materials or strategies in real (not simulated) settings. Institutionalization is the continuing, routine use of the instructional innovation in the structure and culture of an organization.* Both depend on changes in individuals and changes in the organization. However, the purpose of implementation is to ensure proper use by individuals in the organization. The purpose of institutionalization is to integrate the innovation in the structure and life of the organization. Some of the past failures of large scale Instructional Technology projects, such as computers in schools and instructional television, emphasize the importance of planning for both individual and organizational change (Cuban, 1986).

Policies and Regulations. *Policies and regulations are the rules and actions of society (or its surrogates) that affect the diffusion and use of Instructional Technology.* Policies and regulations are usually constrained by ethical and economic issues. They are created both as a result of action by individuals or groups in the field and action from without the field. They have more effect on practice than on theory. The field of Instructional Technology has been involved in policy generation related to instructional and community television, copyright law, standards for equipment and programs, and the creation of administrative units to support Instructional Technology.

Trends and Issues. Trends and issues in the utilization domain often center around policies and regulations which affect use, diffusion, implementation and institutionalization. Another issue associated with this domain is how the influence of the school restructuring movement might affect the use of instructional resources. The role of technology in school restructuring is still evolving. The proliferation of computer-based materials and systems has raised the economic and political stakes for those contemplating adoption. Instructional Technology professionals are now involved in decisions about multi-million dollar expenditures, affecting not just individual teachers and individual classrooms, but whole school districts, colleges, and corporations. The field is increasingly involved in political and economic issues at the level of the whole organization. These factors often have an impact on the ways in which utilization is conducted.

The Domain of Management

The concept of management is integral to the field of Instructional Technology and to roles held by many instructional technologists. Individuals in the field are regularly called upon to provide management in a variety of settings. An instructional technologist might be involved with efforts such as the management of an instructional development project or the management of a school media center. The actual goals for the management activity may vary greatly from setting to setting, but the underlying management skills remain relatively constant regardless of setting.

Many instructional technologists have position titles that imply a clear management function. For example, an individual may be the Learning Resources Center Director at a university. This individual is responsible for the entire learning resources program including goals, organization, staff, finances, facilities, and equipment. Another individual may be employed as the media specialist in an elementary school. This individual may have the responsibility for the entire media center program. The programs administered by these individuals may differ greatly, but the basic skills necessary to manage the program will remain constant. These skills include organizing programs, supervising personnel, planning and administering budget and facilities, and implementing change. Although each author uses slightly different terms, these types of management are described in Chisholm and Ely (1976), Prostano and Prostano (1987), and Vlcek and Wiman (1989).

The management domain evolved originally from the administration of media centers, programs and services. A melding of the library and media programs led to school library media centers and specialists. These school media programs merged print and non-print materials and led to the increased use of technological resources in the curriculum. In 1976 Chisholm and Ely wrote *Media Personnel in Education: A Competency Approach* which emphasized that the administration of media programs

Figure 2.6
The Domain of Management

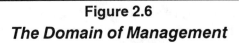

MANAGEMENT

Project
Management

Resource
Management

Delivery System
Management

Information
Management

played a central role in the field. AECT's 1977 definition divided the management function into organization management and personnel management as practiced by administrators of media centers and programs.

As practice in the field became more sophisticated, general management theory was applied and adapted. As projects in the field, especially instructional design projects, became more and more involved, project management theory was applied. Techniques for managing these projects had to be created or borrowed from other fields. New developments in the field have created new management needs. Distance learning depends on successful management because several locations are involved. With the advent of new technologies, new ways to access information are becoming available. As a consequence, the area of information management has great potential for the field.

One theoretical base for information management comes from the discipline of information science. Other bases are emerging from practice in the integrated technologies area of the development domain and from the field of library science. The information management area opens many possibilities for instructional design, especially in the areas of curriculum development and implementation and self-designed instruction.

Management involves controlling Instructional Technology through planning, organizing, coordinating and supervising. Management is generally the product of an operational value system. The complexity of managing multiple resources, personnel, and design and development efforts is multiplied as the size of the intervention grows from small, one-school or -company departments, to state-wide instructional interventions and global multi-national company changes. Regardless of the size of the Instructional Technology program or project, one key ingredient essential to success is management. Change rarely occurs at only the micro-instructional level. To ensure the success of any instructional intervention, the process of any cognitive behavior or affective change must occur in tandem with change at the macro-level. With few exceptions (Greer, 1992; Hannum and Hansen, 1989; Romiszowski, 1981), managers of Instructional Technology programs and projects looking for sources on how to plan for and manage these multiple macro-level change models will be disappointed.

In summary, there are four subcategories of the management domain: project management, resource management, delivery system management and information management. Within each of these subcategories there is a common set of tasks that must be accomplished. Organization must be assured, personnel hired and supervised, funds planned and accounted for, and facilities developed and maintained. In addition, planning for short- and long-term goals must occur. To control the organization the manager must establish a structure that aids decision-making and problem-solving. This manager should also be a leader who can motivate, direct, coach, support, delegate, and communicate (Prostano and Prostano, 1987). Personnel tasks include recruiting, hiring, selecting, supervising and evaluating. Fiscal tasks encompass budget planning, justification and monitoring, accounting and purchasing. Responsibility for facilities entails planning, supporting and supervising. A manager may have responsibility for developing a long range plan. (Caffarella, 1993)

Project Management. *Project management involves planning, monitoring, and controlling instructional design and development projects.* According to Rothwell and Kazanas (1992), project management differs from traditional management, which is line and staff management, because: (a) project members may be new, short-term members of a team; (b) project managers often lack long-term authority over people because they are temporary bosses, and (c) project managers enjoy greater control and flexibility than is usual in line and staff organizations.

Project managers are responsible for planning, scheduling and controlling the functions of instructional design or other types of projects. They must negotiate, budget, install information monitoring systems, and evaluate progress. The project management role is often one of dealing with threats to success and recommending internal changes.

Resource Management. *Resource management involves planning, monitoring, and controlling resource support systems and services.* The management of resources is a critical area because it controls access. Resources can include personnel, budget, supplies, time, facilities, and instructional resources. Instructional resources encompass all of the technologies described in the section on the development domain. Cost effectiveness and justification of effectiveness for learning are two important characteristics of resource management.

Delivery System Management. *Delivery system management involves planning, monitoring and controlling "the method by which distribution of instructional materials is organized . . . [It is]a combination of medium and method of usage that is employed to present instructional information to a learner"* (Ellington and Harris, 1986, p.47). Distance learning projects, such as those at National Technological University and Nova University, provide examples of such management. Delivery system management focuses on product issues, such as hardware/software requirements and technical support to users and operators, and process issues, such as guidelines for designers and instructors. Within these parameters decisions must be made that match the technology's attributes with the instructional goals. Decisions about delivery system management are often dependent on resource management systems.

Information Management. *Information Management involves planning, monitoring and controlling the storage, transfer or processing of information in order to provide resources for learning.* There is a great deal of overlap between storing, transferring and processing because often one function is necessary in order to perform the other. The technologies described in the development domain are methods of storage and delivery.

Transmission or transfer of information often occurs through integrated technologies. "Processing consists of changing some aspect of information [through computer programs] . . . to make it more suitable for some purpose" (Lindenmayer, 1988, p. 317). Information management is important for providing access and user friendliness. The importance of information management is its potential for revolutionizing curriculum and instructional design applications. The growth of knowledge and knowledge industries beyond the scope that today's educational system can accommodate means that this is an area of great importance to Instructional Technology in the future. An important component of the field will continue to be the management of information storage systems for instructional purposes.

Trends and Issues. The trend towards quality improvement and quality management that is seen in industrial settings is likely to spread to educational settings. If so, it will have an influence on the management domain. A synthesis of diffusion of innovations, performance technology and quality management could provide a powerful tool for organizational change. Diminishing availability will challenge managers to make better use of current resources. The marriage of information systems and management will grow and affect Instructional Technology in that management decision-making will be more and more dependent on computerized information.

The Domain of Evaluation

Evaluation in its broadest sense is a commonplace human activity. In daily life we are constantly assessing the worth of activities or events according to some system of valuing. The development of formalized educational programs, many funded by the federal government, has brought with it the need for formalized evaluation programs. The evaluation of these programs required the application of more systematic and scientific procedures.

Curriculum specialist Ralph Tyler is generally credited with promulgating the concept of evaluation in the 1930s (Worthen and Sanders, 1973). The year 1965 saw the passage of the landmark Elementary and Secondary Education Act, mandating formal needs assessments and eval-

---

Figure 2.7
The Domain of Evaluation

EVALUATION

Problem Analysis
Criterion-Referenced
Measurement
Formative Evaluation
Summative Evaluation

---

uation of certain types of programs. Since that time, evaluation has grown into a field of its own, with professional associations (e.g. the American Evaluation Association) and a long list of published books and journal sources.

The publication of Robert Mager's *Preparing Instructional Objectives* in 1962 was an important event in the evolution of evaluation. When preparing for a workshop on programmed instruction, Mager decided to use programmed instruction as an introduction to writing measurable objectives. The program was refined and later published. It is probably one of the most influential publications in the field. Other important contributions historically were the development of the domains of educational objectives (Bloom, 1956; Krathwohl, Bloom and Masia, 1964) and learning classifications (Gagné, 1965).

In the late 1960s Stufflebeam (1969) introduced another approach to evaluation which has now become classic, one which sought "not to prove but to improve" Stufflebeam (1983, p. 118). His model suggested four types of evaluation: context, input, process, and product (CIPP). The four elements in the CIPP model provide for considering information relating to: needs assessment; design decisions which address content and strategy; guidance for implementation; and outcome assessment (Braden, 1992).

With the concern for more formalized evaluation, it became evident that to evaluate one needed to compare results with goals. Thus, the area of evaluation came to encompass needs assessment. With this orientation, Roger Kaufman (1972) presented a conceptual structure for analyzing the appropriateness of teaching goals.

The evaluation domain grew as the educational research and methodology field grew, often in tandem or parallel with that field. Important distinctions between traditional educational research and evaluation became clearer as both areas developed. Scriven (1980) emphasized the difference between evaluation and other types of research. He said that while evaluation is the process of determining the merit, worth or value of a process or product and that this is a research process, the purpose of educational evaluation is different from the purpose of other educational research. The purpose of evaluation is to support the making of sound value judgments, not to test hypotheses.

Evaluation research and traditional research, then, are distinguished by several characteristics. While they often employ similar tools, the ends are different. For traditional research, the end is an increase in knowledge broadly defined. For evaluation research, the end is the provision of data for decision making in order to improve, expand, or discontinue a project, program or product. The aims of traditional research are less time and situation specific because it attempts to uncover principles that apply more broadly. With evaluation research, the object being evaluated is most often a specific program or project in a given context. In other words, much less attention is paid to the question of generalizing the findings to a larger population. While both types of research have common roots historically and share many characteristics and processes, the enterprises in practice are quite distinct.

Evaluation is the process of determining the adequacy of instruction and learning. Evaluation begins with problem analysis. This is an important preliminary step in the development and evaluation of instruction because goals and constraints are clarified during this step.

In the domain of evaluation important distinctions are made between program, project and product evaluations; each is an important type of evaluation for the instructional designer, as are formative and summative evaluation. According to Worthen and Sanders (1987):

Evaluation is the determination of a thing's value. In education, it is formal determination of the quality, effectiveness or value of a program, product, project, process, objective, or curriculum. Evaluation uses inquiry and judgment methods, including: (1) determining standards for judging quality and deciding whether those standards should be relative or absolute; (2) collecting relevant information; and (3) applying the standards to determine quality (pp. 22–23).

As seen in the root concept of the word, the assignment of value is central to the concept. That this assignment is done fairly, accurately, and systematically is the concern of both evaluators and clients.

One important way of distinguishing evaluations is by classifying them according to the object being evaluated. Common distinctions are programs, projects, and products (materials). The Joint Committee on Standards for Educational Evaluation (1981) provided definitions for each of these types of evaluation.

Program evaluations—evaluations that assess educational activities which provide services on a continuing basis and often involve curricular offerings. Some examples are evaluations of a school district's reading program, a state's special education program, or a university's continuing education program (p. 12).

Project evaluations—evaluations that assess activities that are funded for a defined period of time to perform a specific task. Some examples are a three-day workshop on behavioral objectives, or a three-year career educational demonstration project. A key distinction between a program and a project is that the former is expected to continue for an indefinite period of time, whereas the latter is usually expected to be short lived. Projects that become institutionalized in effect become programs (pp. 12,13).

Materials evaluation (instructional products)—evaluations that assess the merit or worth of content-related physical items, including books, curricular guides, films, tapes, and other tangible instructional products (p. 13).

An important distinction here is the separation of personnel evaluation from other categories. In practice, such a distinction is difficult to accomplish. People become personally involved with the development or success of a program or product; even though an evaluator may constantly refer to a separation, with statements like: "People are not being evaluated here. We just want to know if this model program works or not." The people responsible for creating and maintaining these entities are justifiably concerned about the outcomes of the evaluation. In practice, people's effectiveness is often judged by the success of their program or product, regardless of what definitional distinctions one would like to make.

Within the domain of evaluation there are four subdomains: problem analysis, criterion-referenced measurement, and formative and summative evaluation. Each of these subdomains will be explained below.

Problem Analysis. *Problem analysis involves determining the nature and parameters of the problem by using information-gathering and decision-making strategies.* Astute evaluators have long argued that the really thorough evaluation will begin as the program is being conceptualized and planned. In spite of the best efforts of its proponents, the program that focuses on unacceptable ends will be judged as unsuccessful in meeting needs.

Thus, evaluation efforts include identifying needs, determining to what extent the problem can be classified as instructional in nature, identifying constraints, resources and learner characteristics, and determining goals and priorities (Seels and Glasgow, 1990). A need has been defined as "a gap between 'what is' and 'what should be' in terms of results" (Kaufman, 1972), and needs assessment is a systematic study of these needs. An important distinction should be offered here. A needs assessment is not conducted in order to perform a more defensible evaluation as the project progresses. Instead, its purpose is more adequate program planning.

Criterion-Referenced Measurement. *Criterion-referenced measurement involves techniques for determining learner mastery of pre-specified content.* Criterion-referenced measures, which are sometimes tests, also can be called content-referenced, objective-referenced, or domain-referenced. This is because the criterion for determining adequacy is the extent to which the learner has met the objective. A criterion-referenced measure provides information about a person's mastery of knowledge, attitudes or skills relative to the objective. Success on a criterion-referenced test often means being able to perform certain competencies. Usually a cut-off score is established, and everyone reaching or exceeding the score passes the test. There is no limit to the number of test-takers who can pass or do well on such a test because judgments are not relative to other persons who have taken the test.

Criterion-referenced measurements let the students know how well they performed relative to a standard. Criterion-referenced items are used throughout instruction to measure whether prerequisites have been mastered. Criterion-referenced post-measures can determine whether major objectives have been met (Seels and Glasgow, 1990). Curriculum designers and other educators were interested in criterion-referenced measurement before Mager described behavioral objectives (Tyler, 1950). Early contributors to the application of criterion-referenced measurement in Instructional Technology came from the programmed instruction movement and included James Popham and Eva Baker (Baker, 1972; Popham, 1973). Current contributors include Sharon Shrock and William Coscarelli (Shrock and Coscarelli, 1989).

Formative and Summative Evaluation. *Formative evaluation involves gathering information on adequacy and using this information as a basis for further development. Summative Evaluation involves gathering information on adequacy and using this information to make decisions about utilization.*

The emphasis on both formative evaluation in the early stages of product development and summative evaluation after instruction is a prime concern of instructional technologists. The distinction between these two types of evaluation was first made by Scriven (1967); although Cambre has traced these same types of activities to the 1920s and 1930s in the development of film and radio instruction (Cambre, cited in Flagg, 1990).

According to Michael Scriven (1967):

> Formative evaluation is conducted *during* the development or improvement of a program or product (or person, etc.). It is an evaluation which is conducted *for* the in-house staff of the program and normally remains in-house; but it may be *done by* an internal or external evaluator or (preferably) a combination. The distinction between

formative and summative has been well summed up in a sentence of Bob Stake's "When the cook tastes the soup, that's formative; when the guests taste the soup, that's summative" (p. 56).

Summative evaluation is conducted *after* completion and *for* the benefit of some *external* audience or decision-maker (e. g. funding agency, or future possible users, though it may be done by either internal or external evaluators for a mixture. For reasons of credibility, it is much more likely to involve external evaluators than is a formative evaluation. It should not be confused with outcome evaluation, which is simply an evaluation focused on outcomes rather than on process—it could be either formative or summative (p. 130).

In product development, the use of formative and summative evaluations are particularly important at varying stages. At the initial stages of development (alpha stage testing), many changes are possible, and formative evaluation efforts can have wide ranging scope. As the product is developed further, the feedback becomes more specific (beta testing), and the range of acceptable alternative changes is more limited. These are both examples of formative evaluation. When the product finally goes to market and is evaluated by an outside agency, which plays a "consumer reports" role, the purpose of the evaluation is clearly summative—i. e. helping buyers make a wise selection of a product. At this stage, without a wholesale revamping of the product, revision is virtually impossible. Thus, we see that in the development of a product, the uses of formative and summative evaluation vary with the stage of progress and that the range of acceptable suggestions narrows over time.

The methods used by formative and summative evaluation differ. Formative evaluation relies on technical (content) review and tutorial, small-group or large group tryouts. Methods of collecting data are often informal, such as observations, debriefing, and short tests. Summative evaluation, on the other hand, requires more formal procedures and methods of collecting data. Summative evaluation often uses a comparative group study in a quasi-experimental design.

Both formative and summative evaluation require considerable attention to the balance between quantitative and qualitative measures. Quantitative measures will typically involve numbers and will frequently work toward the idea of "objective" measurement. Qualitative measures frequently emphasize the subjective and experiential aspects of the project and most often involve verbal descriptions as the means of reporting results.

Trends and Issues. Needs assessment and other types of front end analyses have been primarily behavioral in orientation through their emphasis on performance data and on breaking content down into its component parts. However, current stress on the impact of context on learning is giving a cognitive, and at times a constructivist, orientation to the needs assessment process. This emphasis on context is evident in the performance technology movement, situated learning theories, and the new emphasis on more systemic approaches to design (Richey, 1993). Consequently, the needs assessment phase is gaining in importance. In addition, many are recommending that the needs assessment phase assume greater breadth, moving beyond concentration on content and placing new emphases on learner analysis and organizational and environmental analysis (Richey, 1992; Tessmer and Harris, 1992). The performance technology movement is also making an important contribution to the new needs assessment emphasis. Performance technology approaches may cause a broadening of the designer's role to include identifying aspects of the problem that are not instructional and working with others to create a multi-faceted solution.

The quality improvement movement will affect the evaluation domain. Quality control requires continuous evaluation including extending the cycle beyond summative evaluation. Confirmation evaluation (Misanchuk, 1978) is the next logical step in the cycle. In a 1993 article Hellebrandt and Russell argue that:

> Confirmative evaluation of instructional materials and learners completes a cycle of evaluative steps in order to maintain performance standards of an instructional system. Following some time after formative and summative evaluation, a team of unbiased evaluators uses tools like checklists, interviews, rating scales, and tests to answer two fundamental questions: first, do materials still meet the original objectives; second have learners maintained their level of competence?

Other researchers are re-examining criterion-referenced measurement techniques. For example, Baker and O'Neil (1985) explore in-depth the issue of assessing instructional outcomes including new directions for criterion-referenced measurement. They present a new model of evaluation adapted to the new technologies. Their model takes into account the goals, intervention, context, information base and feedback loops.

Other areas of great interest are the measurement of higher level cognitive objectives, affective objectives and psychomotor objectives. Research on computerized criterion-referenced measurement will stimulate this domain as will the research on qualitative measures, such as portfolios and more realistic measurement items like case studies and evaluation of taped presentations. Cognitive science will continue to influence this domain in terms of newer approaches to diagnosis (Tennyson, 1990). These areas will be discussed further in Chapter Three.

New technologies have raised further issues in the evaluation domain and created a need for new techniques and methods. For example, attention needs to be directed toward improving the evaluation of distance learning projects. These tend to be evaluated superficially. It is important that evaluation of distance learning cover many aspects, i. e. personnel, facilities, equipment, materials, programming (Clark, 1989; Morehouse, 1987). Reeves (1992) recommends formative experimentation which uses a small scale trial and error approach to study a variable in real life context.

Tessmer (1993) proposes a formative evaluation model which accommodates a 'layers of necessity' approach. This approach takes into consideration the resources and constraints of each project, and attempts to avoid planning layers of formative evaluation which cannot be realistically accomplished within a project.

Eastmond (1991) presents a scenario of an evaluator's dilemma in 2010. In the scenario, the evaluator's role becomes one of questioning data collected by sophisticated information management tools. Duchastel (1987) suggests a triangular procedure of checks and balances on data collected for the evaluation of software. Thus, product review, checklist procedure, user observation and objective data evaluations are used together to give a more complete picture of the software. This approach supports the trend towards a combination of quantitative and qualitative data gathering techniques (Seels, 1993c).

Summary

The five domains of Instructional Technology highlight the diversity of the field. In addition, these domains are complex entities in themselves. This chapter emphasizes the taxonomic nature of the domain structure. One could continue the definition process and develop more specific levels of the taxonomy. The future work of instructional technologists will shape more finite definitions of the subcategories and the areas within them.

Sources of Information

The following sources are suggested for further study of the topics in this chapter. The complete list of references, including those cited in this chapter, can be found at the end of the book.

The Domain of Design

Briggs, L., Gustafson, K. and Tillman, M. H. (Eds.). (1991). *Instructional design principles and applications* (2nd Ed.). Englewood Cliffs, NJ: Educational Technology Publications.

Dick, W. and Carey, L. (1990). *The systematic design of instruction.* (3rd. Ed.) Harper Collins.

Fleming, M. & Levie, W.H. (Eds.). (1993). *Instructional message design: Principles from the behavioral and cognitive sciences.* Englewood Cliffs, NJ: Educational Technology Publications.

Gagné, R.M.; Briggs, L.J.; and Wager, W.W. (1992). *Principles of instructional design* (4th Ed.). Fort Worth, TX: Harcourt Brace Jovanovich, Publishers.

Leshin, C. B., Pollock, J. and Reigeluth, C. (1992). *Instructional design strategies and tactics.* Englewood Cliffs, NJ: Educational Technology Publications.

Seels, B. and Glasgow, Z. (1990). *Exercises in instructional design.* Columbus, OH: Charles Merrill.

Tobias, S. (1987). Learner characteristics. In R. M. Gagné (Ed.), *Instructional technology: Foundations.* (pp. 207–231). Hillsdale, NJ: Lawrence Erlbaum Associates.

The Domain of Development

Alessi, S. M., and Trollip, S. R. (1985). *Computer-based instruction: Methods and development.* Englewood Cliffs, NJ: Prentice-Hall.

Dwyer, F. M. (1978). *Strategies for improving visual learning.* State College, PA: Learning Services.

Gropper, G. (1991). *Text displays.* Englewood Cliffs, NJ: Educational Technology Publications.

Jonassen, D. H. (1988). *Instructional designs for microcomputer courseware*. Hillsdale, NJ: Lawrence Earlbaum Associates.

Kemp, J. E. and Smellie, D. C. (1989). *Planning, producing and using instructional media* (6th Ed.). NY: Harper Collins.

Wileman, R.E. (1993). *Visual communication*. Englewood Cliffs, NJ: Educational Technology Publications.

The Domain of Utilization

Burkman, E. (1987). Factors affecting utilization. In R. M. Gagné (Ed.), *Instructional Technology: Foundations* (pp. 429–456). Hillsdale, NJ: Lawrence Erlbaum Associates.

Canning, T. and Finkel, L. (1993). *The technology age in the classroom*. Wilsonville, OR: Franklin, Beedle & Associates.

Cunningham, W. G. (1982). *Systematic planning for educational change*. Mountain View, CA: Mayfield Publishing Co.

Heinich, R., Molenda, M. and Russell, J. D. (1993). *Instructional media and the new technologies of instruction*. NY: Macmillan Publishing Co.

Morgan, R.M. (1987). Planning for instructional systems. In R.M. Gagné (Ed.), *Instructional technology: Foundations* (pp. 379–396). Hillsdale, NJ: Lawrence Erlbaum.

Rogers, E. (1983). *Diffusion of innovations*. NY: Free Press.

The Domain of Management

Eraut, M. (Ed.). (1989). *The international encyclopedia of educational technology* (Part 5, Distribution and organization of knowledge and resources). NY: Pergamon Press.

Greer, M. (1992). *ID project management*. Englewood Cliffs, NJ: Educational Technology Publications.

Heinich, R. (1991). Restructuring, technology, and instructional productivity. In G.J. Anglin (Ed.), *Instructional technology: Past, present, and future*. (pp. 236–240). Englewood Cliffs, NJ: Libraries Unlimited.

Information power: Guidelines for school library media programs. (1988). Washington, D.C.: American Association of School Librarians and Association for Educational Communications and Technology.

Morris, B.J. et al. (Eds.). (1992). *Administering the school library media center.* New Providence, NJ: Bowker.

Rothwell, W. J. and Kazanas, H. C. (1992). *Mastering the instructional design process.* San Francisco: Jossey-Bass Publishers.

The Domain of Evaluation

Flagg, B. (1990). *The formative evaluation of educational technologies.* Hillsdale, NJ: Lawrence Erlbaum Associates, Publishers.

Morris, L. L. (Ed.). (1978). *Program evaluation kit* . Beverly Hills, CA: Sage Publications. A series developed by the Center for the Study of Evaluation (CES), University of California at Los Angeles. The series includes:

> *Evaluator's handbook*
> *How to deal with goals and objectives*
> *How to design a program evaluation*
> *How to measure program implementation*
> *How to measure achievement*
> *How to measure attitudes*
> *How to calculate statistics*
> *How to present an evaluation report*

Priestley, M. (1982). *Performance assessment in education and training: Alternative techniques.* Englewood Cliffs NJ: Educational Technology Publications.

Rossett, A. (1987). *Training needs assessment.* Englewood Cliffs, NJ: Educational Technology Publications.

Shrock, S. A. and Coscarelli, W. C. C. (1989). *Criterion-referenced test development.* Reading, MA.: Addison-Wesley.

Worthen, B.R. & Sanders, J.R. (1987). *Educational evaluation: Alternative approaches and practical guidelines.* New York: Longman.

Chapter 3

The Sources of Influence on Instructional Technology

Instructional Technology has developed and emerged as a separate field with diverse domains of research and practice. Figure 1.1 in Chapter One portrayed the range of activity encompassed within the traditional boundaries of Instructional Technology—Design, Development, Utilization, Management, and Evaluation. Each of these domains was defined and discussed in Chapter Two.

The range of domains in this field reflects its eclectic nature. Elements of research, theory, and practice from related fields have found their way into the sphere of Instructional Technology by adoption and adaptation. As new influences are felt, they typically dominate for a time and then blend into the existing paradigms, but even when orientations become less dominant, their influence is usually not totally lost in either thought or practice. However, the integration of new ideas occurs within, and reflects, the impact of the broader social and technological contexts of the field.

The Historical Development of the Field

As stated in Chapter Two, the first indication that a field existed was the emergence of visual education, and subsequently audiovisual education, as a concept. Early books by Hoban, Hoban and Zisman (1937) and Dale (1946), assisted by extensive and effective use of media in U.S. military training during World War II, launched the field into legitimacy. Events in other parts of the world also highlighted the importance of media. For example, in Canada the National Film Board, one of the earliest documentary film production agencies, was established in 1939.

Research findings of Wood and Freeman (1929), Knowlton and Tilton (1929) and Carpenter and Greenhill (1956) confirmed the value of media in the process of teaching and learning and helped to establish the field. Later, Fleming and Levie (1976; 1993) summarized much of the earlier media and psychological research and presented their synthesis as guidelines for message design.

Today, the field has encountered the instructional possibilities presented by the computer as a medium of teaching and learning, as well as its use as a tool for integrating a variety of media into a single unit of instruction. In addition, video, which can be two-way and interactive, has largely replaced educational film.

Concurrent with the introduction and development of instructional media as an area of study, the notion of a science of instruction was evolving. Instructional psychologists provided a theoretical foundation which focused on those variables influencing learning and instruction. According to early leaders in the field, the nature of the learner and the learning process itself took precedence over the nature of the delivery methodology.

Some of the early audiovisual specialists referred to the work of Watson, Thorndike, Guthrie, Tolman, and Hull. But it was not until the appearance of Skinner's (1954) work on teaching machines and programmed learning that professionals in the field felt that they had a psychological base. Skinner's work in behavioral psychology, popularized by Mager (1962), brought a new and apparently more respectable rationale for the field. Lumsdaine and Glaser (1960) and Lumsdaine (1964) illustrated the relationship of behavioral psychology to the field, and

Wiman and Meierhenry (1969) edited the first major work that summarized the relationship of learning psychology to the emerging field of Instructional Technology. Bruner (1966), Glaser (1965) and Gagné (1965; 1989) introduced new concepts that eventually led to broader participation of cognitive psychologists. Today, the field not only seems convinced of the importance of the various aspects of cognitive processing of information, but it is placing new emphasis upon the role of instructional context and perceptions of the individual learner.

Perhaps one of the most profound changes in Instructional Technology has come in the expansion of the arenas in which it is typically practiced. Although it began in elementary and secondary education, the field was later influenced by military training, adult education, and post-secondary education, and much of today's activity is in the area of private sector employee training. Consequently, in the current environment, there is increased concentration on issues related to organizational change, performance improvement, and cost benefits.

The principles, products, and procedures of Instructional Technology continue to be vital to school effectiveness, especially in times of school restructuring. Nevertheless, many instructional technologists feel they are not particularly welcome in school environments, nor their ideas especially heeded. The new technologies and new delivery methodologies, however, do offer ways of meeting the special needs of learners and schools. An example of this phenomenon is the emerging role of distance education in all levels of education, from the primary grades through teacher staff development and employee training.

Instructional Technology, and instructional design procedures in particular, are also becoming more common in health care education and training, and non-formal educational settings. Each of these instructional contexts highlights the diverse needs of learners of many ages and interests, and of organizations with many goals. These diverse settings provide laboratories for experimenting with and perfecting the use of the new technologies. The disparate contexts of Instructional Technology also highlight a wide range of organizational and personal values and attitudes. Cultures vary among the different communities, creating new problems, as well as possibilities for new avenues of growth and development in the field.

The Key Sources of Influence

Instructional Technology can be seen as a field primarily concerned with application, even though its principles and procedures are theory-based. The domains of the field have evolved through the concurrent, and at times competing, influence of values, research, and practitioner experience, especially experience with the technologies used in instruction. The field then becomes a child not only of theoretical knowledge, but also of practical knowledge; however, the knowledge base of the profession is understood and used from the particular ethos which predominates among those who call themselves instructional technologists. Each domain is then shaped by:

- its foundational research and theory;
- the prevailing values and perspectives; and
- the capabilities of the technologies themselves.

This chapter will explore each of these areas of influence.

The Influence of Research and Theory

Overview

Instructional Technology has been influenced by theory from several areas. These intellectual roots are often found in other disciplines, including:

- psychology;
- engineering;
- communications;
- computer science;
- business; and
- education, in general.

While research and theory are used by instructional technologists to guide much of their work, it is common for general principles to be translated into the form of models which summarize recommended procedures.

The most influential models describe instructional design procedures. These theoretical areas, while typically having a key relationship to one domain, often impact more than one part of the field. While such relationships have the effect of blurring distinctions between the domains, they also tend to be a unifying force within the field.

Figure 3.1 shows some of the relationships among the theory bases and the domains of the field. This is not intended to be an exhaustive delineation of theories pertinent to Instructional Technology; rather, it shows the manner in which theories support the field and the overlap among domains.

Figure 3.2, on the other hand, shows the relationships between major avenues of research and the domains of Instructional Technology. In many cases, it is possible to directly relate research topics in this figure to a theory base shown in Figure 3.1. For example, message design research relates to and contributes to communication theory; learner characteristic research can relate to motivational theory.

Unfortunately, these tidy relationships are not always present. Some research has not been synthesized or generalized in a theoretical framework. As an example, there is no general theory of media. Consequently, the media effectiveness and media comparison research topics appear isolated from theory, even though these topics relate to a specific domain, and media research has contributed substantially to the development of the field.

Instructional Technology research is eclectic from a methodological standpoint. Driscoll (1984) notes that using a range of research paradigms is typical of a developing science, and therefore ideal for instructional systems research. Consequently, the research base for the field uses not only traditional quantitative research methods, but a variety of alternative paradigms, such as ethnography, developmental and evaluation research, and cost-effectiveness studies.

The following sections will summarize the manner in which specific research and theory have contributed to and influenced the domains of Instructional Technology. It is not intended, however, that the research and theory foundations of each domain will be fully explicated here. *(See Chapter Two for related discussions of each domain.)*

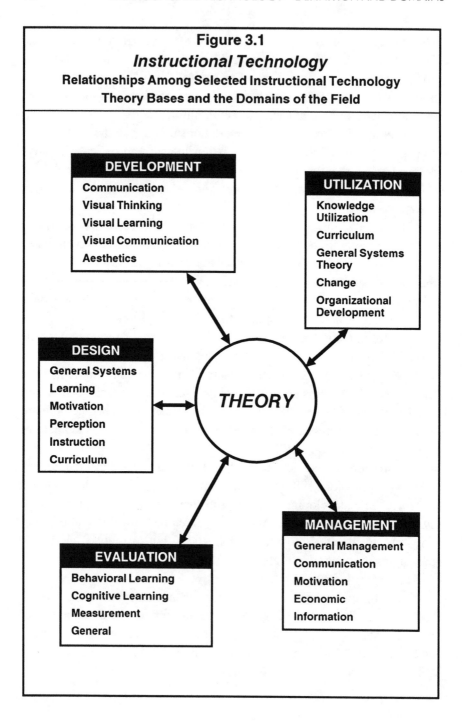

Figure 3.1
Instructional Technology
Relationships Among Selected Instructional Technology
Theory Bases and the Domains of the Field

DEVELOPMENT
Communication
Visual Thinking
Visual Learning
Visual Communication
Aesthetics

UTILIZATION
Knowledge Utilization
Curriculum
General Systems Theory
Change
Organizational Development

DESIGN
General Systems
Learning
Motivation
Perception
Instruction
Curriculum

THEORY

MANAGEMENT
General Management
Communication
Motivation
Economic
Information

EVALUATION
Behavioral Learning
Cognitive Learning
Measurement
General

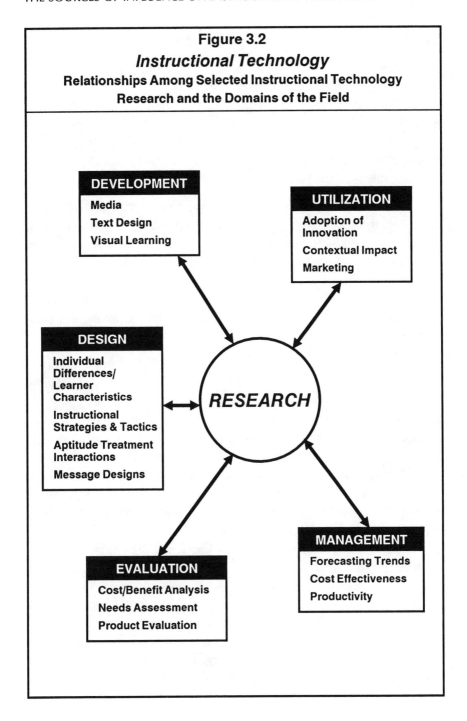

Figure 3.2
Instructional Technology
**Relationships Among Selected Instructional Technology
Research and the Domains of the Field**

DEVELOPMENT
Media
Text Design
Visual Learning

UTILIZATION
Adoption of Innovation
Contextual Impact
Marketing

DESIGN
Individual Differences/ Learner Characteristics
Instructional Strategies & Tactics
Aptitude Treatment Interactions
Message Designs

RESEARCH

MANAGEMENT
Forecasting Trends
Cost Effectiveness
Productivity

EVALUATION
Cost/Benefit Analysis
Needs Assessment
Product Evaluation

Design

A hallmark of instructional design is the notion that its principles and procedures are supported by research. The nature of this research varies from traditional controlled experimentation to developmental research to qualitative analyses of case studies. Even though alternative design perspectives have emerged, all with research support or guided by a distinct theoretical posture, there are key streams of thought that have provided direction to the field. These will be discussed here.

General Systems Theory. General systems theory has been applied to the field through the use of instructional systems design (ISD) models. The allegiance to these models is so widespread that the approach serves as a paradigm that binds the vast majority of instructional designers into a common community. ISD, as a theory, is primarily supported by deductive logic, evaluated practice, and successful experiences. The research base that does exist for systematic design supports the component parts of the design process, i.e., the effects of objectives-based instruction, or the adequacy of the content as analyzed.

Psychological Theory and Research. Instructional design is firmly rooted in learning theory. Traditionally, the behaviorist viewpoint was dominant in instructional design applications. Today, the field stresses applications from cognitive psychology (Polson, 1993), and many are also looking to constructivist principles for further guidance.

The behaviorist is concerned with performance as the only evidence that learning has taken place. There has been a trend within behaviorist research to emphasize the effects of stimulus materials upon the resulting performances of the subjects studied. In contrast, the cognitivists are more interested in changes in what learners know and the structure of their knowledge. They tend to emphasize how one processes new information by examining how one remembers this information. It is a much more internal orientation, as opposed to the external approach of the behaviorists (Lajoie, 1993). The constructivists also are internally oriented. They assert that one's knowledge, and the learning process itself, are rooted in a person's unique interpretation of the world. Such views are determined by one's experience and his or her interpretations of these experiences. This orientation emphasizes the role of context, the context of both the instruction and the transfer situation (Duffy and Jonassen, 1992).

Another major source of psychological influence on instructional design procedures relates to creating and maintaining a motivated learner. The importance of learner motivation has pervaded Instructional Technology from the early emphasis on audiovisual aids as motivators to the current attention given to embedding motivation design into instructional design. For example, Keller (1987a; 1987b) has formulated specific motivation design procedures from a broad base of psychological research. This research addresses topics such as the role of one's expectations and behavior, interests, curiosity, need for achievement, and academic attitudes (Keller, 1979).

Instructional Theory and Teaching-Learning Research. Designers select specific instructional events and activities based upon a variety of factors that impact the teaching-learning process. Each of these key factors also depends upon its own research and theory base. The differences among the designs of various events of instruction are typically attributed to the subject matter, since the vast majority of instructional design models are embedded in the basic assumption that instruction should vary dependent upon the type of learning task being addressed. Subject matter classification is typically based upon one of a variety of taxonomies, including:

- Bloom's (1956) taxonomy of the cognitive domain;
- Krathwohl, Bloom and Masia's (1964) taxonomy of the affective domain;
- Harrow's (1972) taxonomy of the psychomotor domain;
- Gagné's (1985) delineation of the five learned capabilities; and
- Merrill's (1983) definition of content in Component Display Theory.

The general approach to selecting instructional strategies, therefore, begins with classifying the learning task. However, other phases in the design process are also dependent upon the nature of the learning task, including techniques for providing feedback (Smith and Ragan, 1993).

A second key aspect of determining the basic instructional design is the selection of media. This process has held a central role in the field regardless of the complexities and capabilities of the instructional media available. In the 1950s and 1960s, Dale's Cone of Experience (Dale, 1946) was an easily understood model used to explain the levels of concreteness provided by the various categories of media, and it played a role in media selection. *(See the Cone of Experience reproduced in Chapter One, Figure 1.2.)* Specifically, it posited that media could be used to connect concrete and abstract concepts in order to promote learning. Dale's Cone was reflective of John Dewey's experiential philosophy of education. Subsequently, Heinich, Molenda, and Russell (1993) related the various levels of the Cone of Experience to Bruner's scheme of instructional activities—activities seen as abstract, iconic, or enactive. Current media selection models (Reiser and Gagné, 1982; Romiszowski, 1985) tend to emphasize systematic analyses of the instructional setting, content, and learner characteristics.

Designers are also dependent upon the many research findings that validate the use of general instructional methods such as lecture and discussion, cross-age tutoring or small group interactions. In addition, there is an important body of research on the impact and effectiveness of specific instructional tactics such as feedback and reinforcement, drill and practice, or gaming and simulation. There is also a large body of media comparison research that has had the goal of determining the advantages of one teaching medium over another. While this research orientation (as well as the importance of media in the learning process) has been severely criticized (Clark, 1983), others are still supporting additional research of this nature. Kozma (1991), for example, is especially interested in the interactions between the medium of instruction and individual learner characteristics. Such thinking continues the history of aptitude-treatment interaction research and investigations of the impact of individual differences in the teaching-learning process. Ross and Morrison (1989) also continue to advocate media research; they emphasize the value of media replication studies to compare effectiveness and efficiency outcomes.

Communications Theory and Perception-Attention Research. Traditional communications research, especially when combined with established principles of human learning, has had major influence on instructional design, especially micro-design situations such as page layout, screen design, graphics and visual design. Research relevant to perception, and gaining and controlling attention has been of particular importance. Fleming (1987) describes those aspects of attention-getting of most importance to the designer. Specifically, attention is highly selective, typically drawn to things that are moderately complex or novel, and greatly influenced by learner expectations and instructional cues. In addition, Fleming (1987) summarizes the design-relevant characteristics of perception, including organization, comparisons and contrasts, color, proximity, relative value, and information areas of a display.

Research such as this has traditionally been crucial to media design and development, and it currently has impact on new technologies in areas such as screen design, desk top publishing, and design of multimedia instruction. Moreover, it is fundamentally important to the study of visual thinking, visual learning, and visual communication.

Development

The process of developing instruction depends upon design procedures, but the general governing principles are derived from the nature of communication in addition to the process of learning. Specifically, development has been influenced by not only communication theory, but also theories of visual and auditory processing, visual thinking, and aesthetics. In addition, the various specialty areas within the development domain also have separate avenues of influence stemming from research and theory.

Theory Impacting the Domain as a Whole. Individuals working in the early days of audiovisual education realized that their efforts were aimed at the communication of ideas through the new tools that had been embraced by educators. Neophyte educational technologists found a comfortable explanation of what they were trying to do in the theory of Shannon and Weaver (1949). Primarily Shannon and Weaver described the process of getting a message from a sender to a receiver using sensory means. A more popular version of the model was found in Berlo's work (1960) which emphasized the fact that people (not media) were at the heart of the process. This model described a circular relationship between the Sender, the Message, the Channel, and the Receiver, and was commonly called the SMCR model. Schramm (1954), working in the field of mass communications, also applied Shannon and Weaver's work to larger audiences, emphasizing the human behavior aspects of communication.

Individuals in the field continued to flirt with mass communications concepts as they explored the unconventional ideas of Marshall McLuhan (1964) with the expectation that his insights might help explain some of the vagaries of the field. Since mass communications and Instructional Technology use the same media, the mass communications concepts have remained within the boundaries of the field. For example, the research on the effects of television comes from two areas—instructional television and mass media.

In addition, there has been a large amount of micro-level research which has influenced text design and techniques of developing instructional materials using the various technologies. Computer screen design is one example of the current use of micro-level communication guidelines.

The development domain also has been influenced by the visual literacy movement through the application of theories of visual thinking, visual learning, and visual communication. Heinich, Molenda, and Russell (1993) define visual literacy as "the learned ability to interpret visual messages accurately and to create such messages" (p. 73). The underlying assumptions of visual literacy are that a visual language does exist, that people do both think and learn visually, and that people can express themselves visually (Flory, as cited in Tovar, 1988).

Visual thinking theory is useful in generating ideas for visual treatments in the creation of instructional materials. Visual thinking is an internal reaction state. It involves more manipulation of mental imagery and more sensory and emotional association than other stages (Seels, 1993d). Arnheim (1972) describes visual thinking as preconscious, metaphorical thought. Visual thinking calls for the ability to organize images around elements such as line, shape, color, texture, or composition. The elements of visuals are used to make visual statements which have a profound impact on the learning of people of all ages.

Applications of visual learning theories focus on visual design and are incorporated into mediated instruction of all types. In this respect, the principles of aesthetics are also basic to the development processes (Schwier, 1987). Heinich, Molenda, and Russell (1993) identify the key elements of art used in visual design (line, shape, texture, color) and the principles of aesthetic design (arrangement, balance, and unity). However, there are many other lists of visual design elements and principles (Curtiss, 1987; Dondis, 1973). Principles of visual communication also provide basic direction in the development of instructional materials. They are used to guide processes such as graphic design and editing (Pettersson, 1993; Willows and Houghton, 1987).

Research and Theory Impacting the Domain Subcategories. There are four major areas of specialized activity within the development domain—print technologies, audiovisual technologies, computer-based technologies, and integrated technologies. Within each subcategory, preferred production processes and procedures have evolved. The supporting research has tended to be developmental in nature, such as those studies constructed as part of formative and summative evaluations.

A range of techniques has emerged and been refined as a consequence of such research. For example, with respect to print technologies, concepts of readability and techniques for determining the readability level of text material have emerged. The notion of structured writing and its elements has also been applied not only in the design of education and training products, but with other types of communication vehicles, such as memos (Jonassen, 1982).

Within the expanding area of computer-based technologies specific techniques are emerging with the aid of developmental research and practitioner creativity. Programming and authoring techniques are being applied to many settings. Often these bodies of knowledge are used in combination with other more general design theories. The development of distance learning programs may require general communication principles, graphic design principles, interactive learning principles, as well as advanced electronic techniques. The process of developing multimedia, or integrated media, instruction combines principles of both audio and video production, computer-based authoring principles, graphic design principles, and the more fundamental principles of instructional design.

Many of the principles used with respect to the newer technologies are rooted in the early research and theory related to traditional audiovisual technologies. While there has been criticism of the *lack* of a clear theoretical framework of media research (Heidt, 1988), the role of instructional media has always been pivotal in the field. As previously discussed, researchers through the years have conducted numerous experiments known as media comparison studies that attempted to demonstrate the effectiveness of one medium over another, or of mediated instruction over non-mediated instruction. These studies have provided further attempts to refine the media selection process, as well as to validate the use of current technology. More recent research also has addressed the impact of specific media attributes on individual learners and on their approach to information processing.

Research on media (such as instructional film, television, audio tape, and slides) has served as a rich source of information providing direction for effective media development techniques and procedures. It not only has produced general guidelines for effective media use, but also has addressed the issues of specific learner skills and characteristics which facilitate effective use of media.

Utilization

Historically, the notion of utilization connoted aspects of media use to many practitioners in the field, but this domain is currently expanded to include the diffusion and utilization of knowledge, as well as the role of public policy as a mechanism of institutionalization. Outside of Instructional Technology, the study of utilization typically means knowledge utilization, and is influenced by research and theory related to the history and philosophy of science and the sociology of knowledge (Dunn, Holzner, and Zaltman, 1989). These same principles have led to important assumptions by instructional technologists as well.

It is assumed that utilization is constrained by:

- individual frames of reference;
- social conditions;
- problems of the entire receiving system; and

- the actions of communicating parties (Dunn, Holzner, and Zaltman, 1989).

Examples of factors which impact the utilization of instructional processes and materials include learner attitudes toward technology, the learner's independence level, and other factors which create barriers to or facilitate media and materials use in the broader instructional system. Utilization research within Instructional Technology has addressed issues such as the optimal climate for media usage, the impact of media on the economic elements of learning, and the impact of media on learning time (Thompson, Simonson, and Hargrave, 1992). In addition, broader issues of utilization are also being debated and studied within the field of Instructional Technology. Of special interest is the feasibility of widespread use of instructional systems design principles and techniques in school settings (Martin and Clemente, 1990).

Utilization is dependent upon the process of diffusion. In this respect the work of Rogers (1962, 1983) has provided a major influence on understanding the phenomenon of diffusing innovations. As discussed in Chapter Two, the major product of his exploration of the diffusion process was a model broadly based on research concerned with the *adoption* of innovations. This research identified those variables which impacted the reception of new ideas and then described the typical process of an innovation gaining acceptance. The Rogers model is based upon the supposition that there are four main elements operating in the diffusion process—the characteristics of the innovation, communication channels, time, and a social system.

In addition, Havelock's (1971) research on development and diffusion and his social interaction model have emphasized efforts to connect users to sources of new knowledge. The concept of opinion leaders and their importance in the communication process was proposed by Lazarfield and his colleagues in 1944. His research revealed that information flowed to opinion leaders, first as a simple transfer of information; then it flowed from opinion leaders to followers (Lazarfield, et.al., 1944, as cited in Rogers, 1983).

In 1957 Westley and MacLean published a communications model that provided not only for the two step flow proposed by Lazerfield, but also for the role of gatekeepers. Their model explained how dyadic (two person) communication, mass communication, and feedback all played a role in the communication process (Westley and MacLean, 1957, as cited in Burgoon and Ruffner, 1978). Since then the role of the opinion leader has been increasingly identified as important in the general communications process, and especially in communications for the purpose of diffusion of innovations. Both Havelock (1971) and Rogers (1983) emphasize the importance of the opinion leader.

In addition to the role of opinion leaders, few successful applications of Instructional Technology occur without some change in the institutions or organizations in which they are used (Vanderschmidt and Segall, 1985). The past failure of large scale technology innovations highlights the importance of planning for organizational, administrative and individual change (Cuban, 1986). In many of the newer application contexts this orientation is presented as the process of organizational development which was described in Chapter Two. In the domains of the 1994 definition, it is called implementation and institutionalization.

There is a growing body of knowledge concerning the ways in which organizations can better adapt to the challenges of a modern society, with its new markets, technologies, and increasing need for change (Margulies and Raia, 1972). The evolving concepts and techniques have generally emerged from using applications of behavioral science research to achieve individual and organizational change. However, insuring successful implementation of an innovation typically requires that attention also be paid to issues that may not be directly associated with instruction; this circumstance has given rise to the performance technology approach.

Diffusion may be the product of a variety of processes. Seven ways of utilizing research have been identified. For example, it may be the result of an accumulation of convincing research results, or the result of a problem solving process. The political approach to knowledge diffusion, on the other hand, culminates in the formation of policies and regulations (Weiss as cited in Keeves, 1989). This type of diffusion is becoming increasingly important to practitioners, and the research and theory is instrumental in shaping and enacting many regulations critical to this field. For example, there is a major effort to place restraints on showing violence on television and the time and type of commercials shown during children's prime television viewing time.

Molenda (1993) summarizes the theory and components of utilization by proposing that there are at least three *stages* in the process. The relationship between these stages (usage, installation, and institutionalization) is shown in Figure 3.3.

At the simplest end of the spectrum, usage implies the simple, spontaneous or planned, one-time use of an instructional material or technique. On the other hand, installation occurs when the material or technique is embedded in a larger package or instructional system, or the material or technique is considered for permanent (or quasi-permanent) implementation within a structured curriculum of an organization. The third stage of the process is institutionalization. Here there is a conscious effort to embed the instructional innovation (material, technique, or system) into the structure and culture of an organization. Molenda's conceptualization of the stages of utilization strengthens the taxonomic structure of this domain, since his sequence reflects, to a great extent, the order of the subcategories in the utilization domain.

In an effort to provide additional synthesis of the utilization domain's intellectual framework, Molenda (1993) notes that its literature reflects either "the perspective of the *provider*—someone who is attempting to convince others to use an innovation . . . or of the *user*—someone who is a potential adopter of the innovation" (p. 3). From the provider's perspective, the concern is to find ways and means to persuade potential users to become actual users. The change agent would turn to literature or experience from marketing, diffusion of innovations, or perhaps organizational development depending on whether the goal was simple usage, installation, or institutionalization. From the user's perspective, the concern is to select the best available materials or techniques and to find ways and means of employing them as advantageously as possible. The user would turn to literature addressing issues related to pedagogy, materials selection techniques, or the effects of learner characteristics. The research and theory discussed here has been primarily oriented to the provider.

Management

Management concerns within the field of Instructional Technology reflect the influence of behaviorism and systematic thinking as well as

Figure 3.3
Relationship Between Stages in Utilization

INSTITUTIONALIZATION
(embedded in organization)

INSTALLATION
(permanent, in curriculum)

USAGE
(spontaneous, one-time)

Note: Molenda, M. (1993, January 13). The Knowledge Base of the Utilization Domain. Paper presented at the 1993 Annual Meeting of the Association for Educational Communications and Technology, New Orleans, LA.

the more humanistic aspects of communication, motivation, and productivity theories. Management methodologies and theory have been applied to the diverse areas of project and resource administration and coordination, on the one hand, and the more general promotion of change, on the other.

The majority of management principles have emerged from business administration, and little management research and theory construction has been produced by members of the Instructional Technology community. The most profound influence upon the management domain has been from Instructional Technology practitioners, rather than theorists (Greer, 1992). Library and media resource management practice, project management practice, facilities management practice—activity in each of these areas through the years has formed the basis of current techniques.

Project management, as a concept, was "first introduced as an efficient and effective way to assemble, in a short time, a team of people whose combined knowledge and expertise matched up to unique situational and technical demands posed by a given work assignment" (Rothwell and Kazanas, 1992, p. 264). It differs from traditional management concerns to a great extent because the authority stems from knowledge expertise rather than line and staff organization. Consequently, influencing and negotiation techniques assume important roles in addition to typical practices related to planning and controlling time and resources.

Resource management has historically been a key concern of school library media specialists and classroom teachers, both of whom serve as a manager of learning resources. The concept of resources now refers to the broader notion of resources for learning rather than only to audiovisual materials. As such, resources are assumed to also encompass printed materials, environmental resources, and resource persons (Eraut, 1989).

Today there is an additional emphasis in resource management on cost effectiveness within a training environment. Once again instructional technologists are using the theoretical frameworks from other disciplines, such as Henderson and Quandt's (1980) economic theory of resource employment. Exemplifying the nature of management-related theorizing within our field, Becker and Davis (1983) have used the Henderson and Quandt model as a basis for their economic model of industrial training.

This model can be used to help justify the resources expended in an Instructional Technology project.

A natural extension of resource management is the management of delivery systems. Here, the typical concern is with product issues, such as hardware and software requirements, technical support to users and operators, and other operational characteristics of the technology system. This is an emerging area in which practice precedes the theoretical analysis of model applications.

The last component of the management domain is information management. This area is fundamentally influenced by information theory which "provides a way of treating written or spoken language as a series of bits of information . . . provides a way of measuring the information content of a particular sample. It looks at a language as if it is an instrument for handling information without considering the meaning of the content" (Lindenmayer, 1988, p. 312).

Information theory forms the basis for understanding and programming computers. This is pertinent to designing and maintaining computer networks to use for transmission, reception, and storage of information. The applications of information theory, however, are far reaching, as new processes of transmitting information are becoming common place in the workplace. This same phenomenon also occurs in educational institutions, and soon will be in the home. Information theory is also rapidly transforming the manner in which instructional designers work with the development of electronic performance support systems and each of the other management areas of interest. The management of projects, resources, and delivery systems are all influenced by the growing dominance of information management and information theory.

Future conceptualization of the management role of an Instructional Technologist will not only encompass these uses of technology, but will also extend more into human resources management and strategic planning. While much of the orientation may again be that of a behavioral and engineering perspective, motivation theory and change theory having a more humanistic focus may also surface.

Evaluation

Analysis, assessment and evaluation play a pivotal role in the instructional design process and in Instructional Technology itself. In the Worthen and Sanders (1973; 1987) framework presented in Chapter Two, evaluation is seen as a form of research which uses the tools of research to provide the means by which instructional technologists can make complex decisions. Educational evaluation is thus portrayed as a type of disciplined inquiry with an orientation which is primarily:

- systematic;
- criterion-referenced; and
- usually positivistic.

Evaluation has been most commonly associated with the behavioral orientation to instructional design and the related positions generated by general systems theory. General systems theory, which typically guides the overall design process, provides the logic for most evaluation tasks encountered by instructional technologists. Needs assessments, formative and summative evaluations, and criterion-referenced testing are all prompted by the systems approach. They are prompted by the need to create self-regulating systems and a belief in the positive role of feedback.

The birth of instructional design as a behaviorist process resulted in the regular use of behavioral objectives, and the logical extension of objectives-oriented instruction is criterion-referenced testing. At this time, both of these techniques have become entrenched in design practice, even among those who espouse a more cognitive approach. However, both the advantages and disadvantages of objectives-based instruction typically extend to the use of criterion-referenced testing. Nevertheless, essentially all instructional design procedures advocate using criterion-referenced test construction for instructional situations rather than norm-referenced techniques. Some constructivists, however, would object to both of these traditional forms of testing, opting for a completely different approach.

Similarly, needs assessment and other types of front end analyses have been primarily behavioral in orientation. This is evident by the emphasis on performance data and breaking down content into its component parts. Design techniques such as the use of learning hierarchies and job task analyses are clearly behavioral. The expanded needs assessments advocated by performance technologists are also essentially governed by a behavioral stance.

However, currently there is an increased tendency to interject a cognitive, and at times a constructivist, orientation to the various analysis and evaluation tasks in the instructional systems design process. For example, many are now considering the impact of context on learning. This position has important implications for the needs assessment process. Many are recommending that the needs assessment phase assume greater breadth, moving beyond concentration only on content and placing new emphases on learner analysis and organizational and environmental analysis (Richey, 1992; Tessmer and Harris, 1992). Others who also reflect a cognitive orientation are questioning the reliance upon using and measuring specific behavioral objectives because they may not lend themselves to the "largely unique and individual organization of knowledge" (Hannafin, 1992, p.50). Consequently, there are concerns that the product of such instruction is surface, rather than deep, learning (Kember and Murphy, 1990).

Emphases on higher level cognitive objectives is likely to further stimulate this domain especially as evaluation in the cognitive paradigm takes on more diagnostic functions. Cognitive science is influencing ways of diagnosing learning needs during instruction and measuring achievement within the context of meaningful and complex situations. Continued critical analyses and innovations of this type could have important implications for assessment and evaluation procedures as they are traditionally followed in this field.

Values and Alternative Perspectives of the Field

Common Values of the Field

In most fields there are shared values which also serve as a foundation for thinking and practice. These values may result from: similar training or work experiences, an enculturation emanating from the theory bases, or personality characteristics of persons attracted to that discipline.

Instructional technologists, as a community of professionals, tend to value concepts, such as:

- replicability of instruction;
- individualization;
- efficiency;
- generalizability of process across content areas;
- detailed planning;
- analysis and specification;
- the power of visuals; and
- the benefits of mediated instruction.

These unwritten priorities have evolved with the growth of the field. They form a bond which links members of the field. Many are interested in instruction, learning, technology, media, and the design of instruction; however, the Instructional Technology community is united not only by the combination of these interests, but also by traditions and cultures which have tended to solidify these common values and priorities.

Disciplinary values are shaped by the other aspects of the culture—the research and theory, the dominant philosophical positions, the nature of the settings in which applications are made, and especially for this field—the resources available. However, in spite of the existence of common characteristics of the field, there are, nonetheless, a number of prominent alternative views which also shape the work of instructional technologists.

Alternative Perspectives

Instructional Technology is an evolving field. Since technology is, by no means, the sole preserve of this field, Instructional Technology attracts theorists and practitioners from many other fields. In addition, the field contains many subspecialties, each of which may function to some extent as a separate community of scholars and practitioners. As a result, Instructional Technology is a field with many complexities and points of view, in spite of the existence of many shared values.

The concept of alternative paradigms for discovering and verifying knowledge has recently been a major focus in many different disciplines. From a scholarly perspective, these alternative paradigms include the move towards an acceptance of qualitative research methodologies, the introduction of phenomenological research, and a move toward constructivist psychology. Instructional Technology has also felt many of these same influences.

Instructional Technology has tended to position itself as a science, and thus most technologists are oriented toward positivism. The positivist view holds that knowledge is inherently scientific in nature. Objective observation is valued, and a means-end, or cause-effect relationship among aspects of the environment is pursued. The positivist strives for the ability to predict and control outcomes. Experimental, quantitative research is the preferred mode. This philosophy was exhibited in the field through its emphasis on evaluation and research-based theory.

While this orientation is still dominant in much of the field today, there is nonetheless a growing body of alternative views being presented in the field today. These views tend to be either:

- critical examinations of common positions;
- alternative theoretical orientations; or
- alternative foundational philosophies.

Critical Examinations of the Field. Typical of the first body of thought are criticisms of the technology emphasis in the field and the society at large. For example, Striebel (1991) presents the thesis that the computer "is not just another 'delivery system' but an environment that has certain values and biases associated with it" (p. 117). Inherent in these somewhat camouflaged biases is a behavioral orientation that becomes so pervasive that it tends to mitigate against the use of other theoretical orientations. He also questions the feasibility of real learner control in an instructional situation which has been so carefully pre-structured by others.

Since technology is not the sole preserve of instructional technologists, there is also a body of technology criticism presented by theorists and philosophers outside of the field which provides analyses relevant to our profession. McLuhan's explorations of media (1961; 1984) are the most popular. His work provides a framework for questioning the impact of media on society. Bowers (1988) also provides a direct challenge to instructional technologists who argue that technology is totally neutral and can be molded to meet any desired goal.

Alternative Theoretical Positions. Representative of the new theoretical perspectives is constructivist psychology (Duffy and Jonassen , 1991). Constructivisim holds that, while physical reality exists, our only knowledge of that reality comes from interpretation of experience. Meaning does not and cannot exist independent of the person who knows. Learning consists of an on-going process of interpreting our experience and adjusting our interpretations in light of new experiences. Constructivists talk of designing learning environments rather than didactic instructional sequences. These environments are conceived as contexts rich in both expanded knowledge bases, authentic problems and authentic tools for use in the solution of those problems. There is an aversion to a pre-specification of the specific knowledge to be mastered and a similar aversion to the simplification or regularization of content since those processes strip instruction of the required rich context which promotes transfer.

Another perspective, not entirely incompatible with the constructivist orientation, is promoted by those who highlight the strengths of situated learning. "Situated learning occurs when students work on 'authentic tasks' whose execution takes place in a 'real-world' setting. It does not occur when students are taught decontextualized knowledge and skills" (Winn, 1993, p. 16). When one emphasizes situated learning, the logical extension is to see learning as active, as ongoing, as judged more in terms of application than in terms of acquisition (Brown and Duguid, 1993). Winn (1993) has shown how instructional design tenets can be applied to attain the benefits of situated learning, and in doing so points out the importance of "teaching at a level of generality that allows for application in multiple settings" (p. 17). He also cites the barriers often imposed by technology when striving to introduce flexibility in instructional designs.

On a more applied basis the performance technology movement (Geis, 1986) is also presented as an alternative perspective of Instructional Technology, or to some as a clear alternative to the field. It is a mindset which recognizes individual and organizational realities when solving on-the-job performance problems. There are many similarities between traditional Instructional Technology and performance technology, including an adherence to a systems approach, reliance upon needs assessment, and focusing attention on the cause of performance problems.

However, performance technologists are more likely to identify with the business needs and goals of their organizations, rather than learning goals. Performance technology, as an approach to problem solving, is a product of a variety of theoretical influences, including cybernetics, behavioral psychology, communications theory, information theory, systems theory, management science, and the cognitive sciences (Geis, 1986). It represents the typical pattern of multiple theoretical influences common in this field.

Performance technologists do not always design instructional interventions as a solution to their problems. Performance technologists are as likely to turn to improvements in incentives, job design, personnel selection, feedback, or resource allocation as interventions, as they are to design instructional interventions. It is difficult to conceive of using performance technology principles outside of the confines of an organization, while Instructional Technology principles could be used in any instructional situation, be it within a formal organization or not.

Alternative Philosophies. Finally, post-modern philosophy is encouraging critical analysis of the very foundation of traditional beliefs and values of the field. The post-modern perspective emphasizes the notion that Instructional Technology is as much an art as a science. Hlynka (1991) has described post-modernism as "a way of thinking which celebrates the multiple, the temporal, and the complex over the modern search for the universal, the stable, and the simple" (p.28). It presupposes that one philosophy, or one theory, is not better than another; all exist together and should be used together. Post-modernists recognize and find intellectual stimulation in a rich potpourri of knowledge-generating systems and tend to view any single definition of the field (such as the one being presented here) as a way of stifling the creativity needed to stimulate productive inquiry and practice.

There are many implications of the post-modern philosophy for design practice as well as design theory. Primarily, this orientation promotes the use of new design paradigms rather than relying upon systematic design models. This includes an increased reliance upon aesthetic paradigms and any model which emphasizes the complexities of a situation. There is a fundamental rejection of reductionist, simplifying approaches. In addition, there is a rejection of the more traditional view that change of any type is a gradual, cumulative process. Because the use of multiple theoretical approaches is advocated, post-modernist philosophy favors applications that result in open, flexible systems as opposed to closed, structured, and rigid systems (Hlynka, 1991). There is a corresponding concern with instruction that focuses only upon declarative knowledge, instruction which isolates learners from the surrounding "real" world, and instruction that stifles the learner's curiosity.

The Impact of Technology

In addition to the impact of research and theory, Instructional Technology as a field has been, and increasingly will be, shaped by the influence of technology and technology advancements. This occurs in spite of the continuing efforts to define the field in terms of process, as opposed to hardware. From the early applications of programmed instruction in the mid 1950s, to the success of educational television using instructional design principles (e.g. *Sesame Street*) in the late 1960s, to the introduction of the Apple II microcomputer in 1977, technology has influenced growth in this field (Seels, 1989).

Currently, the new technologies are providing the impetus for much of the current advancement in both disciplinary theory and practice. This is what Salomon (1992) calls the 'bottom-up' pattern of theory development. These new technologies provide avenues of development which address many current issues, including the need to:

- devise principles for adapting instruction to unique situations,
- devise new approaches to interactive instruction, and
- devise instruction for non-formal learning environments.

Technology's impact has been described by distinguishing between the effects *of* technology and the effects *with* technology (Salomon, 1992). This dichotomy can be used to examine the general influence of technology on the field. When exploring the effects of technology one can consider the growing range of delivery system possibilities and their impact on instruction and learning. New technologies present the prospects, for example, of creating increasingly realistic stimuli, providing for quick access of large quantities of information, rapidly linking information and media, and removing the barriers of distance between instructor and learners and among learners themselves (Hannafin, 1992). Creative, skilled instructional designers can build instructional products which take advantage of the cability to:

- to integrate media;

- to incorporate almost unlimited learner control; and even

- to redesign themselves to adapt to individual needs, backgrounds, and work environments.

These improvements in technology are changing the nature of practice within the field. They also have implications for research as well as subsequent theory expansion. For example, learning environments using the new technologies provide an opportunity for researchers to more completely describe the role and impact of complex and extensive interactivity in learning, and of aptitude-treatment interaction effects.

However, when considering the effects *with* technology, the questions take a different orientation. They focus upon the effects of an intellectual partnership between the learner and technology, upon the role of technology-enhanced environments on higher-order thinking and other cognitive processes (Salomon, 1992). Technology, from this point of view, becomes a force which encourages cognitively-oriented theory and practice

In addition to providing a wider range of instructional media, technology is also influencing practice in the field by providing computer-based tools to support the design tasks themselves (Gustafson and Reeves, 1990). Automated design workstations and expert design systems will probably increase designer productivity and reduce the constraints posed by detailed, systematic design procedures, without sacrificing the quality attained by using traditional instructional systems design procedures. Merrill, Li, and Jones (1990) have suggested that these innovations will result in a second generation of instructional design.

Summary

This chapter has examined the primary forces which have shaped the field of Instructional Technology—research and theory, values and alternative paradigms, and the technology itself. The field has been influenced through these forces as it evolved from a visual education movement to a more complex field applied in a wide range of education and training environments. These forces have been felt as the field moved from a concern with books and pictures to a concern with computers and interactive multimedia. The forces have been felt as the field expanded from a small group of academics and practitioners to a large, international community of instructional technologists.

Sources of Information

The following sources are suggested for further study of the topics in this chapter. The complete list of references, including those cited in this chapter, can be found at the end of the book.

Hlynka, D. and Belland, J. (Eds.). (1991). *Paradigms regained: The uses of illuminative, semiotic and post-modern criticism as modes of inquiry in educational technology.* Englewood Cliffs, NJ: Educational Technology Publications.

Jonassen, D.H. (Ed.). (forthcoming). *Handbook of research on educational communications and technology.* New York: Scholastic Publishing Company.

Reigeluth, C.M. (1983). *Instructional-design theories and models: An overview of their current status.* Hillsdale, NJ: Lawrence Erlbaum Associates, Publishers.

Richey, R.C. (1986). *The theoretical and conceptual bases of instructional design.* London: Kogan Page.

Saettler, P. (1990). *The evolution of American education technology.* Englewood, CO: Libraries Unlimited, Inc.

Thompson, A.D.; Simonson, M.R.; and Hargrave, C.P. (1992). *Educational technology: A review of the research.* Washington, D.C.: Association for Educational Communications and Technology.

Chapter 4

The Practice of Instructional Technology

Instructional Technology has developed through consistent interaction between theory and practice. At times, theory has provided direction for practice, and at other times practice has preceded theoretical analysis. This phenomenon is not unusual for a distinctly applied and practical profession.

The influence of diverse theoretical stances was explored in Chapter Three. Instructional Technology is somewhat unique in that it also relies upon models to supplement theory. The most generally used models in the field are procedural in nature, and the vast majority of these models guide the design processes. While these procedural models have a theoretical basis, most also summarize successful practice or respond to the unique characteristics of a given setting.

Instructional Technology practice has influenced, to a great extent, the evolution of the field and, therefore, has had considerable impact on how the field itself has been defined. Moreover, practice has had more influence than theory on the manner in which the field is viewed by those outside of the field.

The Elements That Shape
Instructional Technology Practice

While practice is often shaped by models and foundational theory, the practice of Instructional Technology is also greatly influenced by the many elements which facilitate or constrain the *use* of such models and theory in the workplace. These elements include:

- the type of instructional content;
- the nature of the learner;
- the organization in which instruction occurs;
- the capabilities of available tools; and
- the expertise of the practitioner.

Instructional Technology techniques and procedures, especially those related to instructional design, are presented as generic models with variations dependent upon the type of subject matter to be taught and, to a lesser extent, the prerequisite skills and background of the learner. However, as with any practical field, the needs and priorities of the organization coupled with the resources and constraints of the instructional setting have as powerful an influence upon practice as do the content demands which tend to be more theoretically established, or even learner needs which are often subsumed under organizational or content needs.

The dimensions of Instructional Technology practice tend to expand as the capabilities of the available technologies increase. Clearly, the introduction of the microcomputer into education and training has dramatically changed the nature of practice in the field, and as computers become more commonplace and more powerful the possibilities for the field have multiplied in an exponential fashion.

As with any field, the quality of practice is determined to a great extent by the skills and expertise of the practitioners. Such expertise has evolved through the years as a function of the many changes in the field, both theoretical and practical. It is also a function of the nature of the positions practitioners assume in the workplace. These positions have been expanding as the benefits of the field become more obvious in a variety of organizations.

This chapter will discuss the impact of practice on the evolution of Instructional Technology. It will address the role of the work setting, the jobs themselves, and the expertise of the professionals in defining current patterns of practice. The ethical framework of the field will also be examined in terms of its influence upon Instructional Technology practice. In addition, this chapter will summarize the historical relationship between practitioner activity and the manner in which the field has been defined.

The Context of Instructional Technology Practice

The various communities of practitioners influence the development of beliefs, values, and priorities in a field. Changes in these beliefs and values are precipitated by both the goals and the resources of a particular work environment. Such impact is particularly significant in Instructional Technology because of the major changes in the work settings of instructional technologists in the past quarter century.

The Scope of Instructional Technology Practice. Typically, graduates of Instructional Technology programs find employment in a variety of work settings. These are shown in Figure 4.1.

The expanding range of settings in which instructional technologists work has had profound impact on the field. Of primary importance has been expansion into the world of private sector training. In most geographical areas, training jobs now specifically call for advanced training in Instructional Technology or a related field. Ely (1992) cites the trend in many areas for instructional development to be practiced more in nonschool settings than in schools. This trend began over a decade ago, and appears to be continuing. Nevertheless, school media specialists are still standard in most K-12 institutions and commonly influence curriculum design and implementation.

From the perspective of many in the field, the more dramatic change has not been so much in terms of a shift to training applications, but rather the expansion of Instructional Technology practice throughout the world. In some cases the international arena is a reflection of the worldwide structure of many American corporations; however, this does not account for all activity. Foreign corporations and ministries of education have supported the expansion of Instructional Technology, often by

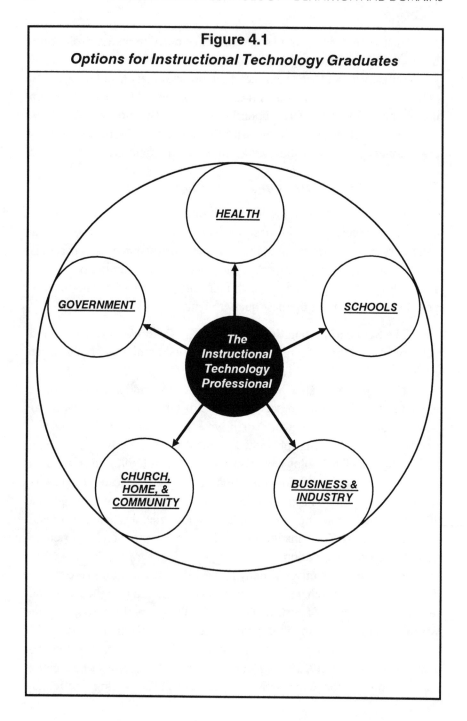

Figure 4.1
Options for Instructional Technology Graduates

encouraging advanced study in this area. Developing countries are finding educational direction from this field. In addition, some countries such as Canada and the Netherlands have substantial Instructional Technology academic programs in their own colleges and universities. Moreover, there is a solid, and growing, base of international research and literature.

This dramatic change in the practice of Instructional Technology has had little impact on the basic structure of the field. The five general domains of the field continue to be relevant to *each* work context. What the employment setting does impact are the resources used, the type of content addressed, and at times the processes applied. These variations may impact role, function, or product.

Another feature of present day work in this field is the fact that many groups have incorporated the applications of technology into their work. As a consequence technologies—even the instructional technologies—are not the interest of this field exclusively. Systems engineers, computer programmers, teachers and academics in many content areas— all have become interested in technology and its uses.

Practice Variations Among Work Settings. Because the business and industrial training arena predominates in some areas, there is a new emphasis in the field on topics such as:

- skill-oriented instruction and subsequent transfer of training;
- content-centered, rather than learner-centered instruction;
- front-end analysis and instructional systems design;
- distance learning technologies;
- the nature of the adult learner; and
- performance technology.

Training environments are often the arenas in which much of the current high-end technology product development occurs. This is due primarily to the fact that private corporations frequently devote more resources to technology than individual schools, or even entire school districts, in the K-12 environment. Moreover, very large corporations can spread their technology investments across a large number of trainees and still be cost efficient on a per student basis.

The training environment also tends to emphasize productivity and reducing the design cycle time. These pressures are leading to the development of electronic performance support systems and new approaches to design and development in the search for more efficient techniques (Dick, 1993; Wager, 1993). However, at times there are also instances in which critical phases, such as evaluation and follow-up, are de-emphasized or eliminated altogether in order to save time and money.

School settings have other needs which impact the practice of Instructional Technology in these environments, including:

- flexible, teacher-controlled instruction;
- meeting the comprehensive needs of students;
- instruction that does not rely on extensive front-end design; and
- assessment and evaluation

Because of the typically greater instructional autonomy of teachers in school settings, as compared with training environments, there are often problems implementing highly structured instructional systems. In addition, it is not uncommon for some teachers to believe that systematic procedures and technology-based instruction is inhumane. Consequently, the applications of Instructional Technology in school settings usually incorporate more opportunities for teachers to make on-the-spot decisions to accommodate special student needs or special events. Even though the typical K-12 situation has fewer technology resources than a corporate setting, there is often a wider variety of instructional strategies employed than is the norm in a shorter-term employee training situation. Finally, even though there are severe shortages of time and monetary resources in public education, there is usually a greater regard for assessment and evaluation procedures in schools than in the typical business setting (Seels and Glasgow, 1991).

It is not surprising that the field has had some difficulty using exactly the same procedures in these two settings without adjustments (Gustafson, 1993), even though there is still a general belief in the validity of generic procedures which transcend setting constraints. Nonetheless, Instructional Technology principles are applied to a wide variety of teaching environments creating a rich practice field, even though there are some resulting tensions.

The Jobs of Instructional Technologists

Jobs of instructional technologists are usually determined as much by the structure and goals of a particular work setting as they are by the function of the position. Seels and Glasgow (1990) have described the job market first by distinguishing between the roles of researcher and practitioner. While researchers in academic settings may be concerned with any domain of the field, they typically specialize in one (or perhaps two) areas of interest. In schools or training environments, most researchers in those organizations are engaged in evaluation research.

Practitioners also may be concerned with any domain of the field, but here too, school-based professionals tend to specialize in a more limited sphere. While there are generalists, the broad scope of Instructional Technology typically prohibits high levels of expertise by a single individual in all domains of activity. This is true for both theorists and practitioners alike. Most instructional technologists have jobs that demand specialized skills in one or two areas—design, and development of certain technologies, or media utilization, for example.

Figure 4.2 shows Seels and Glasgow's (1990) more complete conceptualization of the roles of instructional designers. Here roles are shown to be a function of the major job category, work setting, and the type of product produced. Hence, one might find an instructional designer working in government primarily upon specific computer-based instructional modules, for example. In addition, the jobs demand a specified level of expertise—(I) basic, (II) intermediate, or (III) advanced. It is possible to extend this framework to the field as a whole with some modifications. Practitioners may be managers, for example, in which they are concerned with all domains on a general level, but with the utilization and management domains specifically.

Job titles themselves have little consistency from organization to organization, even within the same work setting. In the school setting, persons with instructional design expertise may be teachers, principals, or curriculum specialists. In the training environment, persons with instructional design expertise are more likely to be called designers, but they may have other titles as well. Rothwell and Kazanas (1992) identify alternative job titles as performance technologist, instructional developer,

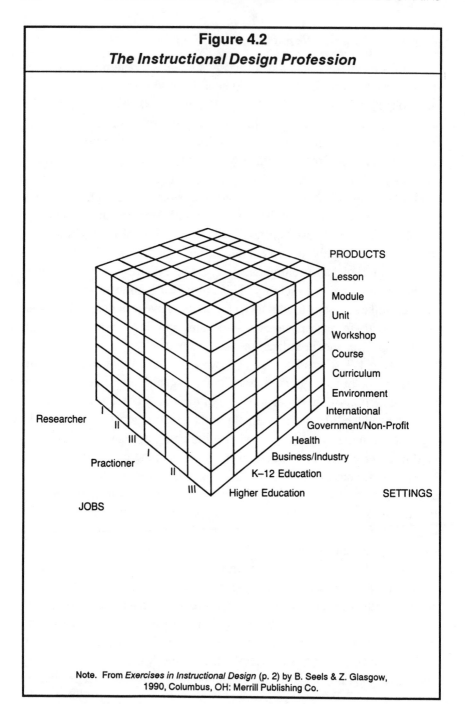

Figure 4.2
The Instructional Design Profession

Note. From *Exercises in Instructional Design* (p. 2) by B. Seels & Z. Glasgow, 1990, Columbus, OH: Merrill Publishing Co.

project supervisor, education specialist, employee educator, trainer, instructional technologist, or instructional systems specialist.

The most stable job titles tend to belong to the more traditional functions within the discipline, those of school media personnel. The school library media specialist and now the computer coordinator are among the most commonly understood positions. In so many other situations, one must examine the actual duties of a position to determine whether the job is actually that of an instructional technologist. To qualify, the position (regardless of its label) must relate to one or more of the domains of the field. Typically, this job will deal with either instructional products, instructional processes, or both.

The Role of Practitioner Expertise

Formal Training and Re-training. In many situations, today's instructional technologists are more skilled than those of past years. More practitioners have received formal training, usually at the graduate level. In 1991 there were 195 master's and 6th year degree programs in the field, and 63 doctoral programs in the United States alone. However, the number of academic programs here has appeared to stabilize after considerable growth (Ely, 1992). The nature of training in the average program has changed to keep current with the new technologies and the new settings in which graduates are employed. Seels (1993b) notes that academic programs are "struggling with how to add topics such as instructional strategies, project management, summative evaluation, and learner characteristics while expanding computer-assisted instruction into integrated media and telecommunications into distance learning . . . " (p. 22). The extent to which these programs can quickly respond to both the theoretical and technological changes in the field, as well as to the changes demanded by practitioners, will determine the levels of expertise new instructional technologists will bring to the workplace.

Furthermore, practicing instructional technologists will continue to develop their skills and expertise through their work activity outside of the scope of formal training programs. This is characteristic of this field because of the rapid growth in new technologies, and it accounts for the proliferation of seminars, continuing education courses, and workshops—

often at the heavily-attended association annual meetings. Maintaining current levels of expertise is a constant problem in the field, especially in private sector training where many persons still have acquired their background only in an informal manner. While the need to keep up-to-date is most often associated with knowledge of the newer technologies and command of the design process, it is also an issue with respect to other rapidly expanding theoretical developments.

Certification of Professional Competence. With the expansion of Instructional Technology, the various associations have tackled the task of developing and agreeing upon a list of core competencies for key practitioner jobs, primarily those in the employee training arena. The related issue of certification of professional competence has also been addressed. Both AECT's Division of Instructional Development and the National Society for Performance and Instruction (NSPI) established similar tasks forces to begin such work, and their efforts were soon merged in the formation of a Joint Certification Task Force in 1977.

In addition to providing a basis for certification, the task force felt the competencies could be used for:

- self-assessment and professional growth;
- establishing common terminology;
- academic program development;
- aiding employers in identifying qualified practitioners; and
- providing a basis for defining the field (Task force on ID Certification, 1981).

This work is continued by the International Board of Standards for Training, Performance, and Instruction (IBSTPI) which was formed as a not-for-profit corporation in 1984 with the approval and encouragement of AECT and NSPI. The issues, however, are complex. While many support the notion of voluntary certification, there are those who fear that such a process will paralyze the field and the preparatory programs in the universities and colleges by restricting the exploration of new ideas and new technologies (Boothe, 1984). Others see certification as a "standard-setting device that assures quality in the field" (Coscarelli, 1984, p. 22).

Today, the certification issue is often seen as an element of the quality movement in American industry. Certification is being proposed as one way of limiting variability, a way of ensuring quality performance and quality instructional products. However, there is still much controversy surrounding the certification issue.

Some see the certification of instructional designers and trainers as comparable to the traditional right of the state to certify classroom teachers or to endorse specialty areas in education, such as school library media specialists, instructional technologists, or computer coordinators. These regulations have had both positive and negative consequences. On the positive side, teacher certification has ensured a basic level of formal preparation, and it has provided for minimum components in that training. A primary example would be requiring that teachers have had supervised classroom experience with children prior to assuming a position with full responsibilities. On the negative side, some see certification standards as the source of increasing bureaucratization of the preparation of teachers which simply adds requirements as a result of pressures from interested parties rather than basic needs.

While certification is typically *required* for teachers, currently few have suggested that certification of Instructional Technology professionals in the training arena be mandatory. Although there has been pressure to require the certification of technology specialists in school settings, with few exceptions only certification of the school library media specialist is commonly mandated at this time.

Certification of academic programs in the field, however, has been the responsibility of NCATE (National Council for Accreditation of Teacher Education). It recognizes Instructional Technology as a knowledge base for both teacher preparation programs and for advanced professional study in education. Instructional Technology programs are reviewed through the auspices of AECT, which approves standards, trains reviewers, and issues the final decisions. Approved Instructional Technology programs, thus, contribute to the overall accreditation of a college of education. There has traditionally been a close relationship between the definition and domains of the field and the NCATE accreditation standards, and the 1994 definition is the basis of the newest NCATE guidelines for reviewing Instructional Technology programs (Caffarella, Earle, Hanclosky, and Richey, 1994)

The Ethics of Instructional Technology Practice

Codification of Ethical Standards

A key facet of any profession is the recognition and enforcement of a standard set of ethical practices. These standards then provide another factor which shapes daily practice within a field. AECT has had a code of professional ethics and procedures for dealing with ethical issues since its formation as an association a quarter of a century ago. Moreover in its previous role as part of the National Education Association, the Division of Audio Visual Instruction (DAVI), the association was also concerned with a formalized codes of ethics. *(See Appendix C for a copy of the current AECT Code of Ethics.)* The fact that AECT took the initiative to develop an ethical code was due in part to the advocacy of James Finn (1953) who saw a codification and vigorous enforcement of professional ethics as one of the six criteria of a profession. Since the code was approved, the Committee on Professional Ethics of AECT has been charged with conducting an annual review of the code, resulting in adjustments and revisions over the years (Welliver, 1989).

This activity was fortuitous, given the attention society is currently placing on ethical issues in a variety of settings. Ethics is impacting such diverse arenas as politics, sports, finance, academic research, and manufacturing. The dictionary definition of ethics is "a set of moral values, those principles of conduct governing an individual or a group." These standards of conduct serve as a more abstract source of direction for daily practice. They are, nonetheless, a vital part of establishing the norms of professional behavior in any field.

Ethical Concerns of the Profession

Because of the rapid technological change which is occurring, ethical norms also are being changed, and new ones established and promulgated. The issues confronted are far-reaching. Some topics are obvious, such as the appropriate use of duplication technologies, including not only print, audio and video, but also computer-based duplication. These standards impact new copyright laws and 'fair use' procedures. In addition, activities of computer 'hackers', such as illegally gaining entry into data bases, and creating and disseminating computer viruses, are posing new problems. These issues are being addressed in the courts, as well as in codes of ethics.

The new technologies have created other ethical issues which are less apparent to many and more subtle in their impact. For example, the question of equity in access to educational opportunities can be an issue with respect to technology. Since the effective use of technology in education often requires systemic change in order to provide access to new hardware, software, and innovative learning processes, there is a greater possibility of creating a bipolar society by widening the gap between the 'haves' and the 'have nots'. This poses both an ethical and practical dilemma. In addition, automation, robotics, and artificial intelligence may present ethical questions relative to the application of these advances in educational systems.

These and other ethical concerns may become even more complicated when other technological advances come to fruition. For example, medical technologies may provide methods of enhancing memory, facilitating learning or altering human perceptions and understanding. In these situations it will be more difficult to determine what is appropriate behavior and what might have a long-term negative impact. The code of ethics provides direction for daily practice and a basis for understanding and interpreting the ethical implications of a variety issues which may confront today's practitioners.

The Role of Practice as an Influence Upon the Evolution of Instructional Technology

Instructional Technology has moved from being viewed as a craft, to a profession, and now a field of study. This evolution has paralleled its growth from primarily technician-level practice in the workplace to professional activity requiring more advanced knowledge and preparation, and then to a field with its own distinct bodies of scholarly research and practitioner expertise. This evolution has been described in a series of key studies of the field, as well as in attempts to define the scope and functions of the field.

The Jobs in Instructional Media Study of 1970

During the late 1960s the Department of Audiovisual Instruction of the National Education Association (the precursor of AECT) conducted an analysis of Instructional Technology practice at that time. This project was undertaken as a way of analyzing the field and, in effect, provided a history of practice to that point. The report of this project, *Jobs in Instructional Media* (Wallington, et al.,1970) and became known as the JIMS report.

Foundations of the Study. The JIMS study was based upon two separate orientations. The first was the notion of a functional job analysis. This technique, developed by Sidney A. Fine of the Upjohn Institute for Employment Research, involves identifying the complete array of tasks in a specific job. Such tasks are then grouped in terms of whether they pertain to data, people, or things. Each category is further sub-divided into functions which can be described by their level of difficulty and the corresponding amount of instruction required to perform that function.

In addition to the functional job analysis techniques, the JIMS study was greatly influenced by a model of the domains of Instructional Technology which had been developed in the Media Guidelines Project of the Teaching Research Division of the Oregon System of Higher Education. Figure 4.3 shows the domains of Instructional Technology as presented in the JIMS report. This chart is essentially the same as the model developed in Oregon. This view equates the *domains* of the field with the *functions* performed by practitioners. It is an idea which has been embedded in most prior definitions of the field (AECT, 1972; AECT, 1977), as well as in this current definition. One distinction is that *previously* the functions of practitioners determined the domains of the field. In the 1994 definition, the domains are established as areas of the knowledge base and the functions of practitioners are subsequently classified into the relevant domains.

Influence and Extensions of the JIMS Report. One conclusion derived from the JIMS report was that a very high percentage of jobs in the field actually involved paraprofessional tasks, such as equipment operation. Consequently, the project expanded to systematically cluster-

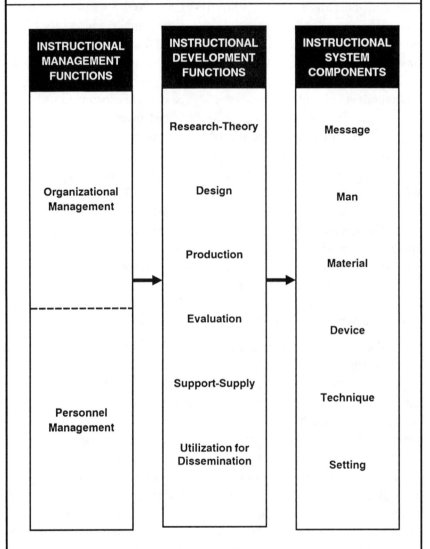

Figure 4.3

The Domains of Instructional Technology as Presented in the JIMS Report

INSTRUCTIONAL MANAGEMENT FUNCTIONS	INSTRUCTIONAL DEVELOPMENT FUNCTIONS	INSTRUCTIONAL SYSTEM COMPONENTS
	Research-Theory	Message
Organizational Management	Design	Man
	Production	Material
	Evaluation	Device
	Support-Supply	Technique
Personnel Management	Utilization for Dissemination	Setting

Note: From *Jobs in Instructional Media* (p. 12a) by C. J. Wallington et al., 1970, Washington, D.C.: AECT.

related job tasks to provide the basis of a career ladder. The JIMS report, therefore, provided one basis for the field to develop into a profession.

However, the report also provided the base for other work which analyzed the nature of the field. AECT received a contract from the National Center for Educational Statistics to compile and clarify terminology related to the field. The resulting handbook of terminology was based upon the "changes in the concepts, processes, techniques, equipment and materials which comprise the field" (Association for Educational Communications and Technology, 1975, p. iii). This document was predicated upon the nature of practice as described in the JIMS report.

A second extension of the JIMS report was Chisholm and Ely's (1976) examination of the functions of media personnel. A major thesis of that book is summarized by the model presented in Figure 4.4 which relates user needs to the jobs of media personnel. That book also further developed the career ladders suggested by the JIMS report.

Although the 1977 AECT definition of the field modified the domain model used in the JIMS report, the classification of functions remained essentially the same. The 1977 definition, therefore, extends the application of the functional job analysis approach to describing a field.

The Relationships Between the 1994 Definition and Practice

The current definition of Instructional Technology is presented as a reflection of both theory and practice. The domains represent the knowledge base of the field in addition to providing the major scheme for classifying the specific manner in which this knowledge is applied in the workplace. Even though the names of the domains themselves denote a process, each domain first must be expressed as forms of activity to solidify the connection to the world of practice. For example, sample activities associated with the design domain might include conducting a content analysis, or making a job aid. In keeping with the overall definition, the activities within each domain may relate to either instructional processes or instructional resources. These relationships are shown in Figure 4.5.

In effect, these process or product-related activities become the *functions* of a particular domain.

There are many professional competencies demonstrated by instructional technologists when their work is associated even with only a single

Figure 4.4
Functions Performed by Media Personnel in Relation to the User

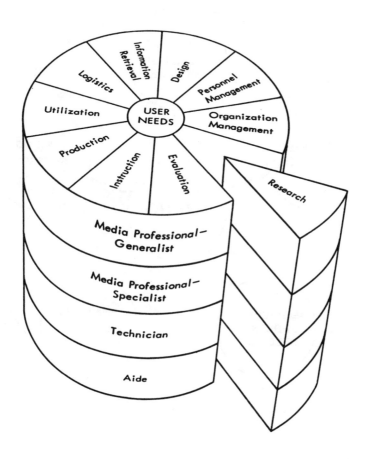

Note. From *Media Personnel in Education: A Competancy Approach* (p. 44)
by M. E. Chisholm & D. P. Ely, 1976, Englewood Cliffs, N.J.: Prentice-Hall, Inc.

Figure 4.5

The Relationship of the Domains to the Activities of the Field

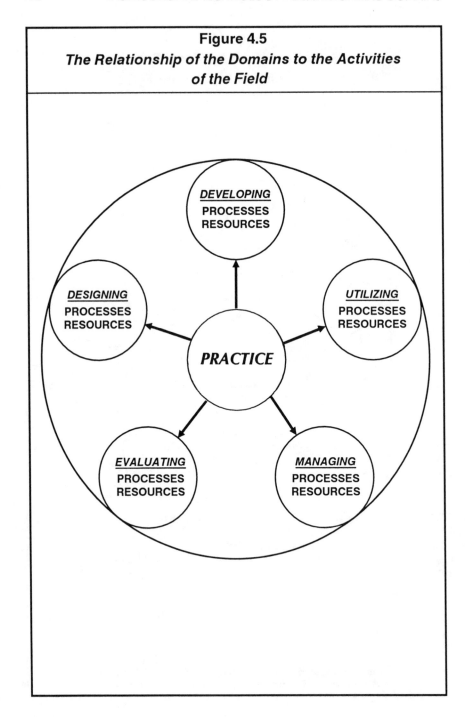

domain. Moreover, there are job titles associated with the same area of competence and performance. As any field expands there typically is a corresponding growth in the jobs, competence, processes and resources associated with each facet of that field. Instructional Technology is no exception. A result of this growth in the field, there has been an increase in job titles, as well as in the total number of jobs. The average levels of expertise demonstrated seem to have grown, and certainly the range and nature of competence has expanded to complement the expansion of technology itself.

Growth in a field, especially rapid growth, can stretch or even exceed the traditional boundaries of that field. In a sense this entire definition process is an effort to set and test such boundaries. The nature of the growth in Instructional Technology practice over the past quarter century seems to reaffirm both the 1994 definition and its five-domain structure. The attempt is to provide a framework that will also accommodate *future* growth in the practice of Instructional Technology, a framework that can subsume new job activities, new professional competencies, new technologies, and newly devised processes.

Summary

The 1994 definition of the field characterizes Instructional Technology as both theory and practice. This chapter has described the field from the orientation of practice. Currently, the practice of Instructional Technology is influenced by the context of the workplace, the range of jobs typically available, and the expected level of expertise of those trained in the various aspects of the field. In addition, practice is shaped by the prevailing ethical standards in the profession. It is clear that the future growth of the field will continue to be shaped by practice, as well as by the expansion of its intellectual framework.

Sources of Information

The following sources are suggested for further study of the topics in this chapter. The complete list of references, including those cited in this chapter, can be found at the end of the book.

Anglin, G.J. (Ed.). (1991). *Instructional technology: Past, present, and future*. Englewood, CO: Libraries Unlimited, Inc. (Part 6—Certification and Professional Development).

Educational media and technology yearbook, Educational Media and Technology: The Year in Review. (An annual section.) Englewood, CO: Libraries Unlimited, Inc. and ERIC Clearinghouse on Information Resources and the Association for Educational Communications and Technology.

Eisenberg, M.B. (1991). *Trends and issues in library and information science*. Syracuse, NY: ERIC Clearinghouse on Information Resources, Syracuse University. (Published bi-annually.)

Ely, D.P. (1992). *Trends in educational technology*. Syracuse, NY: ERIC Clearinghouse on Information Resources Syracuse University. (Published bi-annually.)

Finn, J.D. (1953). Professionalizing the audio-visual field. *Audio-visual communication review, 1*(1), 6–17.

International Board of Standards for Training, Performance, and Instruction. Chicago: IBSTPI

Instructional Design Competencies: The Standards (1986).

Instructor Competencies: The Standards (Vol. I, 1988; Vol. I, 2nd. Ed.; 1993; Vol. II, 1992).

The Training Manager Competencies: The Standards (1989).

Performance & Instruction, 23(1). February, 1984 Theme Issue on Professional Certification.

Training (The Magazine of Human Resources Development), Industry Report: An Overview of Employee Training in America, (An Annual Report in the October issue.)

Chapter 5

Implications of the Definition of Instructional Technology

In Chapter One it was argued that a new definition of Instructional Technology was needed to reflect the growth and diversity of the field today, as well as to serve as a catalyst for creativity and further change. This premise is consistent with Ely's (1983) position that "definitions do not create a field but, rather, help to explain its functions, purposes and roles to those within and those outside the area" (p. 2). This definition effort has the further goal of encouraging the development of a more cohesive community of scholars and practitioners amid extreme diversities of philosophy, job, and work context. This chapter will more specifically examine the role and implications of this particular definition in a rapidly changing field.

The Definition and Its Role in a Growing Field

The Development of a Distinct Field

Inherent in this document is the assumption that Instructional Technology is a separate field of study, a separate branch of knowledge. While it has functioned as a field for many years, and recently as a profession, its more mature status is relatively new to the larger society. This maturity can be examined in terms of professional concerns and clear theoretical boundaries. The definition of Instructional Technology is not only influenced by these dimensions of maturity, but correspondingly the definition provides further impetus for additional growth of the field.

A profession has been characterized by Finn (1953) in terms of its:

- body of theory and research;
- intellectual technique;
- application to practical affairs;
- sizable training and certification requirements;
- enforced ethics; and
- association and communication among members.

Through the years, the field of Instructional Technology has substantially met these criteria, and in the process has developed a sizable body of its own theory, and has broadly applied these principles in a variety of settings. These developments have been documented in Chapters Three and Four.

The expansion of Instructional Technology practice is widely recognized. To a great extent this has paralleled the expansion of technology itself. Whether the field has progressed to the point at which the *bulk* of its theoretical growth is within its own parameters, dealing with its own issues, and advanced by its own scholars is a debatable issue. This is the heart of the discussion regarding the disciplinary maturity of Instructional Technology. Most would agree that the design domain is more mature than the other domains in this respect, since the majority of the theory building and a large portion of the research in Instructional Technology have been directed toward aspects of design. Consequently, even though the intellectual roots of instructional design are derived from the theory of other fields of study, instructional design is now being advanced by a large body of research and theory which is unique unto itself. We need to replace the body of knowledge from other fields with our own knowledge base in each of the five domains. This is the direction and goal of future intellectual growth of the field.

The Evolution of the Definition

The 1994 and the 1977 definitions both stress that Instructional Technology is a comprehensive design and development process used to solve instruction and learning problems. In both definitions Instructional Technology is viewed as a field with a systematic orientation. Yet there is still a concern in some quarters that Instructional Technology is considered to be only the "things of learning" as proposed by Armsey and Dahl (1973), even though this does not seem to be a current issue in the literature of the field. The 1994 definition is now consistent with both the theory and the practice of the field, even though the concept of Instructional Technology as a hardware-oriented profession is still common when speaking to the general public or to those not schooled in the area.

A more critical issue is that of obtaining agreement among the scholars and practitioners of the field on those problems that fall within the scope of Instructional Technology and distinguishing them from those that rightfully belong to other fields. This task is important to a definition, since fields are bound by the nature of the problems which they address. In a mature discipline, there is agreement on whether problems, even new problems generated by a changing society, are pertinent to that field of study and practice. Such decisions are not difficult if the conceptual boundaries of the field are clear. They also are not difficult if the definition of the field is widely accepted and understood at almost an intuitive level. The conceptual boundaries of Instructional Technology can be established by using the structure suggested by the five domains of the field, since these reflect the major areas of practice and specialization. The validity of the definition and the uniqueness of the field then depends to a great extent upon the clarity and comprehensiveness of the domains.

The growth of the definition of Instructional Technology parallels, to some extent, the changing views of the domains of the field. For example, the domain of instructional development as presented in the 1977 definition has grown into three separate domains—design, development, and evaluation—in the 1994 definition. This evolution was the result of the increased activity and importance of these component activities and processes in both theory and practice.

These definition changes have been essentially of an evolutionary, rather than revolutionary, nature. This gradual type of change reflects an element of stability and common understanding among instructional technologists. Fundamentally, this stability reflects the field's commitment to the use of instructional systems design models as the preferred orientation to creating and managing learning environments. In addition, the importance of mediation and visualization to the instructional process is commonly assumed. These shared understandings are reminiscent of Kuhn's description of a paradigm as an "implicit, unvoiced, and pervasive commitment by a community of scholars to a conceptual framework" (Shulman, 1986, p. 4). Kuhn (1962) further asserted that the use of a dominant paradigm in a field is characteristic of disciplinary maturity.

In spite of the general consensus on these fundamentals, there are a growing number of alternative perspectives and approaches. These have been discussed in Chapter Three. Do these alternative explanations and perspectives of the teaching-learning process enrich or splinter the field? Does the framework of the definition and the domains encompass these alternative theoretical positions?

While any disciplinary definition reflects the growth in a field, it could also be argued that *premature* definition can narrow a field intellectually, thus preventing or restraining continued growth. For example, the definition and domains of Instructional Technology as presented here reflect the elements of a systems approach to education. Some might argue that this position can have the effect of limiting the field and suppressing creative problem solving. It can inhibit formation of additional alternative perspectives. The desirable definition, therefore, is one that identifies the boundaries of the field, but does not constrict the thinking of its members. It is hoped that the 1994 definition will function in this manner.

The Definition and Its Role in Communication

Elements That Promote Communication

Shulman (1986) concludes that "the ability to communicate is a central definer of community membership" (p. 4). This ability to communicate is an outgrowth of :

- common training and enculturation;

- common conceptual values and goals; and

- common experiences.

These are all antecedents to membership in a professional community.

Formal training enhances entrance into a profession and communication with others by providing a foundation in the literature and the principles and practices of a field. It explains the knowledge base of the field. It promotes superior practice on the job. It further provides a sense of history, a common set of definitions, and entry into the debates and controversies of the field. Formal training also tends to establish consensus on the problems and paradigms of the discipline. In summary, formal education and training promote a common understanding of the definition of the field.

Many of the pioneers in Instructional Technology received their initial training within other fields, such as psychology, engineering or communications. Such a "family tree" provides a rich academic culture, and promotes the notion that Instructional Technology is an intellectual descendent of other areas of study, but this history also contributes to the continued debate regarding the nature of the field.

Today, current leaders are more likely to have received their introduction to the field from university graduate programs in Instructional Technology. This is almost certainly true for academic leaders and is becoming increasingly true for practitioner leaders. As this entry route becomes routine, there will be even more common understanding of the knowledge base and the boundaries of the field. Another consequence of common professional preparation is a preponderance of common educational values in the field. These background similarities significantly contribute to the development of a common culture, as well as effective communication within the community of Instructional Technology scholars and practitioners.

However, common background experiences also provide a sense of community within a field. Herein lies one of the major contributors to the apparent confusion regarding a definition of this field. There are many occupational settings in which one can apply the principles of Instructional Technology. Each type of setting has a culture of its own, and the diverse cultures can create barriers to communication among Instructional technologists. Perhaps some communication difficulties within the profession need not be attributed to a lack of common definitions, but rather to the impact of multiple communities and multiple cultures among Instructional Technology practitioners.

A Sense of Community

In Finn's 1953 characterization of a profession, he asserted that communication is facilitated by association among professionals. In essence, association creates the sense of community. In addition to association among practitioners who work in a given environment, there are also many formal professional associations in the field of Instructional Technology. Some of these, like the Association for Educational Communications and Technology, encompass many communities of interest, and its members come from a variety of occupational communities. Others, like the International Visual Literacy Association, focus on one area of interest even though its members come from many other communities. When professionals from multiple-work communities and multiple-interest communities associate, there is a far greater chance of communication difficulties than when they are bound by a more narrowly focused interest.

With the emergence of Instructional Technology as a broad but distinct field, it becomes important to link these many communities of instructional technologists to facilitate the communication needed to reach common goals. Common definitions facilitate this end, especially a common definition and understanding of the nature of the field. The definition, however, must be broad enough to encompass the many interests and specialties present in the field. This is one function of the five domains and their various components. In a sense they should provide a "home" for every member of the larger professional community. Given this larger professional group, it should be easier to promulgate standards, codes of ethics, and policy positions, as well as knowledge and technical expertise among the various communities of Instructional technologists.

Professional identification is more than attaching a label to one's self. It is ensured and nourished by a clear sense of direction facilitated by an understanding of the knowledge base of the field, as well as by experience working and associating with others with a similar background. While common definitions of a field do not *guarantee* this sense of identification with a field, such identification is difficult to acquire without them. Moreover, this sense of community and identification is often further dependent upon the breadth of disciplinary definitions and the extent to which they leave room for diversity and creative growth.

The Definition and Its Role in Agenda-Building

The Development of an Agenda for Research and Practice

Growth and development within a field are not typically products of chance. Instead they are more likely to be the result of concrete agendas. These are the specific agendas of either influential leaders in a discipline, or more abstract agendas which reflect the intellectual and social climate of the times. Cobb and Elder (1983), when discussing political agendas, indicate that "The content and dynamics of agenda-building are necessarily a function of the larger social, political, and economic context in which this process is embedded. That context is constantly changing, creating new constraints and altering old ones" (p. 188).

In the history of Instructional Technology, there have been important social forces and events which have influenced the field's agenda. One example is the impact of the Russian *Sputnik* on American educational reforms. Other forces influencing the development of Instructional Technology were the military and industrial demands for quick, effective training. Intellectually, the profound impact of the theories of Robert Gagné on the conditions of learning and the far-reaching influence of the behavioral objectives emphasis also served as a context for the growth of Instructional Technology. The rapidly developing technologies in our society are of both social and intellectual significance for Instructional Technology.

These forces operate on a disciplinary agenda, shaping general approaches to research and theory construction, as well as techniques and principles of practice in the field. At times the influence of agenda-setting forces are obvious. Technological advancements are the clearest example. There are others, however. Constructivism is being felt in a broad range of disciplines, within education and other unrelated disciplines as well.

Political forces are demanding an emphasis on testing. Social forces are emphasizing the impact of diversity on learning.

Agendas guiding growth and change are both written and unwritten. Written agendas are found in legislative funding guidelines. Agendas which are unwritten, but just as influential, are apparent in curriculum changes in university programs. They are also apparent in the final selections of presentations at the annual conventions of professional associations. The definition of the field presented here also can have implications for agenda-setting in Instructional Technology. If the definition is widely accepted and incorporated into the culture of the field, it can have implications for both research agendas and practice agendas alike. These implications are apparent in those aspects which are *different* from the 1977 definition. These differences emphasize the new directions in which the field has moved or is likely to move. It is through these differences that the definition has the potential to serve as a part of the agenda-building process of the field.

Implications for New Professional Agendas

The general areas of difference between the 1977 and the 1994 definitions are:

- the change in name of the field;
- the change in primary orientation of the activities; and
- the changes in the domains.

Herein lie the key sources of influence on the direction of growth and development in the field.

The change in name is on the one hand the most obvious change and, on the other hand, the least important. The rationale for the change has been discussed in Chapter One. The new name emphasizes the major changes in the arenas of practice in this seventeen-year period between the two definitions. In the 1970s, concerns of the schools and the education of children still dominated the field. Today, there is a much wider range of environments in which our professionals work. This has led both researchers and practitioners to be concerned with learners of all ages, with diverse types of content, and with the constraints presented by assorted organizational settings. These varied applications of the general principles and practices of the field require new theory and new research. Such a need is likely to continue for some time.

The second key difference relates to the primary orientation of each of the past definitions as summarized in Chapter One. In 1977 the field was defined essentially as a process. It had a problem solving focus, and even though the strong theoretical roots were discussed, the definition itself was practice oriented. By contrast, the 1994 definition is specifically oriented toward *both* theory and practice. The field is presented more as an area of knowledge and study which can be applied in practical situations. The direction is provided for development into a full discipline in its own right. This change implies the need for increased research and theory construction unique to this field and decreased reliance upon the products of the research and theory of other fields.

The most profound changes, however, relate to the new configuration of domains and the new delineation of the components of each domain. These changes are extensive. In 1977 there were three domains—instructional management, instructional development, and instructional systems. Today, there are five domains, each with four components. These have been described in detail in Chapter Two.

Each domain of the 1994 definition needs to have its own base of research and theory rather than relying primarily on the knowledge of other areas of study. The research bases of the domains are uneven in this respect. There are areas which are barely developed, and others which are well developed. These undeveloped domains and domain components have the greatest implications for new research and practice agendas in the field.

Summary and Conclusions

The 1994 definition of Instructional Technology provides further clarification of the intellectual boundaries of the field, and identifies and emphasizes the connections and dependencies among the domains. It is a stipulative definition which not only describes what the field is today, but prescribes what research is needed for tomorrow. It is intended to facilitate the development of the field and to promote communication among professionals in the community of instructional technologists.

Even though the definition highlights the boundaries of the field, it is not intended to narrow the field or limit the creativity of its members. Instructional Technology has always been viewed as much an art as a science. This characteristic is celebrated, for the creativity of instructional technologists is more likely to maintain the viability of the field than the construction of another definition.

Glossary of Terms

The glossary which follows includes the key terms used in this book. It is not intended to be an exhaustive list of terms important to the field. For a more extensive representation of Instructional Technology and its five domains, one could use this list in conjunction with the more specialized glossaries listed in Appendix A.

Anchored Instruction   A technique of situating instruction in a variety of real-life settings [often simulated] to aid reflection, transfer, and higher level problem solving (Cognition and Technology Group at Vanderbilt, as summarized in Richey, 1993a, p. 19).

Aptitude-Treatment Interaction   Differential interaction between learner aptitudes and instructional treatments.

Audiovisual Aids   Instructional materials or media that rely on both hearing and vision for their effects, but loosely used to describe virtually all instructional materials and media other than conventional printed materials (Ellington and Harris, 1986, p. 17).

Audiovisual Technologies   Ways to produce or deliver materials by using mechanical or electronic machines to present auditory or visual messages.

Authoring   Using an authoring language or system to design and develop instruction.

Authoring Language   A computer language which is specifically designed for developing computer-assisted instruction [and which] requires [the user to have] some knowledge of computer programming (Schwier, 1987, p. 171).

Authoring System   A computer program which is designed for computer-assisted instruction development. Procedures are pre-defined and require little or no programming knowledge on the part of the user (Schwier, 1987, p. 171).

Behavioral Psychology   The school of psychology which holds that all behavior of an organism can be explained in terms of stimulus-response bonds (Ellington and Harris, 1986, p. 21).

Certification   Official endorsement of professional competence.

Code of Ethics   Principles intended to aid members of the field individually and collectively in maintaining a high level of professional conduct.

Cognitive Psychology   A branch of psychology devoted to the study of how individuals acquire, process, and use information (Heinich, Molenda and Russell, 1993, p. 442).

Competency   Knowledge, skills, or attitudes which the student can demonstrate at a pre-determined level.

Computer-Based Technologies   Ways to produce or deliver materials using microprocessor-based resources.

Conceptual Models   Models that define, explain, and describe relationships among variables . . . a product of a synthesis of the related research and knowledge base. They can take various forms; they can be narrative descriptions, or taxonomies for example, or mathematical formulations, or visualizations . . . (Richey, 1986, p.24, 27).

Conditions of Learning   The external and internal circumstances that affect learning.

Conditions of Learning (external)   Specific and unique events that facilitate learning (Gagné and Driscoll, 1988, p. 83), especially those which pertain to the stimuli that are external to the learner such as the timing, sequence and organization of the presentation (Gagné, Briggs, and Wager, 1992).

Conditions of Learning (internal)   Specific and unique events that facilitate learning (Gagné and Driscoll, 1988, p. 83), especially those which pertain to the states of mind that the learner brings to the learning task; in other words, they are previously learned capabilities of the individual learner (Gagné, Briggs, and Wager, 1992, p. 9).

Confirmation Evaluation   The process of determining whether learners have maintained their level of competence and materials remain effective.

It occurs continuously after a period following formative and summative evaluation.

Constructivism   A school of psychology which holds that learning occurs because personal knowledge is constructed by an active and self-regulated learner who solves problems by deriving meaning from experience and the context in which that experience takes place.

Cost-Effectiveness   A technique for jointly considering the costs and outcomes of something in order to make a decision (Doughty, 1988, p. 2).

Criterion-Referenced Measurement   Techniques for determining learner mastery of pre-specified content.

Delivery System   The method (a combination of media and support systems) by which distribution of instructional materials is organized and employed to present instructional information to a learner (Ellington and Harris, 1986, p. 47).

Delivery System Management   Involves planning, monitoring and controlling "the method by which distribution of materials is organized." It is "a combination of medium and method of usage that is employed to present instructional information to a learner." (Ellington and Harris, 1986, p. 47).

Design   The process of specifying conditions for learning; also a domain in the field of Instructional Technology.

Development   The process of translating the design specifications into physical form; also a domain in the field of Instructional Technology.

Developmental Research   The systematic study of designing, developing and evaluating instructional programs, processes and products that must meet the criteria of internal consistency and effectiveness. See also Evaluation Research.

Diffusion of Innovations   The process of communicating through planned strategies for the purpose of gaining adoption.

Dissemination   Deliberately and systematically making others aware of a development by circulating information (Ellington and Harris, 1986, p. 51).

Distance Education   Any instructional situation in which the learner is physically distant from the point of origination, characterized by limited access to teacher and other learners (Heinich, Molenda and Russell, 1993, p. 443).

Distance Learning   See Distance Education.

Dynamic Visuals   Visual images that are perceived as moving.

Educational Technology   See Instructional Technology.

Effectiveness   The extent to which the intervention accomplishes the purpose or achieves the ends desired.

Efficiency   Economical pursuit of ends through use of resources.

Elaboration   Provide[s] detailed information that links a new concept with relevant prior knowledge. Elaborations can use either deductive [expository] or inductive [experiential] processes (Leshin, Pollack, & Reigeluth, 1992, p. 206).

Electronic Performance Support System (EPSS)   A combination of hardware and software components which provides an 'infobase,' expert system, job aids and tools and other elements to support performance of tasks.

Evaluation   The process of determining the adequacy of instruction and learning; also a domain in the field of Instructional Technology.

Evaluation Research   Research that gathers data for decision making in order to prove, improve, expand, or discontinue a project, program or project.

Expert System   A computer program, assembled by a team of content experts and programmers, that teaches a learner how to solve complex tasks by applying the appropriate knowledge from the content area (Heinich, Molenda and Russell, 1993, p.444).

Formative Evaluation   Gathering information on the adequacy of an instructional products or programs and using this information as a basis for further development.

Formative Experimentation   Research which uses a small scale trial and error approach to study a variable in a real life context.

Front End Analysis   Accomplishment of the early stages of the design process, such as analysis of needs, goals, and objectives, and organizing the course units (Briggs, 1977, p. xviii).

Functional Job Analysis   A technique for determining the complete array of tasks performed in a job by grouping in terms of data, people and things and then identifying the associated level of difficulty and the amount of instruction needed.

Functions of the Field Tasks and roles performed by professionals in the field.

Implementation Using instructional materials or strategies in a real (not simulated) setting.

Inductive Learning A teaching[/learning] strategy that proceeds as follows: immersion in a real or contrived problematic situation, development of hypotheses, testing of hypotheses, arrival at conclusion (the main point). Also known as the discovery method. (Heinich, Molenda, & Russell, 1993, p. 443).

Information Management Involves planning, monitoring and controlling the storage, transfer or processing of information in order to provide resources for learning.

Installation Using an instructional material, strategy or program in a permanent or semi-permanent fashion usually by embedding it in the curriculum.

Institutionalization The continuing, routine use of an instructional innovation in the structure and culture of an organization.

Instruction Intervening in order to facilitate learning.

Instructional Technology The theory and practice of design, development, utilization, management and evaluation of processes and resources for learning.

Instructional Strategies Specifications for selecting and sequencing events and activities within a lesson.

Instructional System The total 'package' of materials, tests, student guides, and teacher guides that is needed to reach the goals for any instructional unit, course, or curriculum, along with all supporting activities and processes required to operate the system as it was designed to be operated (Briggs, 1977, p. xxi).

Instructional Systems Design (ISD) An organized procedure for developing instructional materials or programs which includes the steps of analyzing (defining what is to be learned), designing (specifying how the learning should occur), developing (authoring or producing the material), implementing (using the materials or strategies in context), and evaluating (determining the adequacy of instruction).

Integrated Learning System (ILS)   A set of interrelated computer-based lessons organized to match the curriculum of a school or training agency (Heinich, Molenda and Russell, 1993, p. 445).

Integrated Technologies   Ways to produce and deliver materials which encompass several forms of media under the control of a computer.

ISD   See Instructional Systems Design.

Iterative   Steps are repeated and revisions made as new information is revealed at a later step (Seels and Glasgow, 1990, p. 39).

Knowledge Diffusion   The effective transmission of knowledge from those involved in research and development to those who have use for such knowledge (Keeves in Eraut, 1989, p. 582).

Learner Characteristics   Those facets of the learner's experiential background that impact the effectiveness of a learning process.

Learning   A relatively permanent change in a person's knowledge or behavior [or attitudes] due to experience (Mayer, 1982, p. 1040).

Macro-Design   A reference to using the ISD process. Also used to refer to the development of large units of instruction, such as programs and curricula.

Management   Involves processes for controlling Instructional Technology practice including planning, organizing, coordinating and supervising.

Mastery Learning   A systematic approach to instruction based on students performing to a pre-specified criterion level on a given unit of instruction before moving to the next unit of instruction (Dick and Carey, 1990, p. 311) See Criterion-Referenced Measurement.

Materials Evaluation (instructional products)   Evaluations that assess the merit or worth of content-related physical items, including books, curricular guides, films, tapes, and other tangible instructional products (Joint Committee on Standards for Educational Evaluation, 1981, p. 13).

Media Utilization   Is the systematic use of resources for learning.

Message   A pattern of signs (words, pictures, gestures) produced for the purpose of modifying the psychomotor, cognitive, or affective behavior of one or more persons (Fleming and Levie, 1993, p. x).

Message Design   Planning for the manipulation of the physical form of the message (Grabowski, 1991, p. 206).

Micro-Design The design of instructional strategies. Also used to describe the development of small units of instruction, such as lessons and modules.

Motivation The magnitude and direction of behavior . . . the *choices* people make as to what experiences or goals they will approach or avoid, and the *degree of effort* they will exert in that respect (Keller, 1983, p. 389).

Motivation Design [planning instructional interventions that] are interesting, meaningful and appropriately challenging [by specifying strategies likely to lead to] interest, relevance, expectancy and satisfaction (Keller, 1983, p. 395).

Multimedia A collection of materials in several different media or a single work designed to be presented through the integrated use of more than one medium (Ellington and Harris, 1986, p. 111).

Needs Assessment A systematic process for determining goals, identifying discrepancies between goals and the status quo, and establishing priorities for action (Briggs, 1977, p. xxiv).

Objectives-Oriented Instruction Teaching sequences which are designed so that learners will achieve pre-defined goals and learn pre-defined content.

OD See Organizational Development.

Organizational Development (OD) A complex educational strategy intended to change the beliefs, attitudes, values, and structure of organizations so that they can better adapt to new technologies, markets, and challenges, and the dizzying rate of change itself (Bennis, 1969, p. 2).

Performance Technology Is the process of selection, analysis, design, development, implementation, and evaluation of programs to most cost-effectively influence human behavior and accomplishment (Geis, 1986, p. 1).

Phenomenological Research Investigation based upon an epistemological perspective that advocates studying human behavior only from the subjects' point of reference. Objective knowledge is consequently rejected, and data from individual cases are meaningful in their own right without being grouped with similar observations.

Policies and Regulations The rules and actions of society (or its surrogates) that control the diffusion and use of instructional technology.

Positivism (Logical) A philosophy asserting the primacy of observation in assessing the truth of statements of fact and holding that metaphysical and subjective arguments not based on observable data are meaningless.

Post-Modernism Is a way of thinking which celebrates the multiple, the temporal, and the complex over the modern search for the universal, the stable, and the simple. Other synonyms for postmodern include breakup, irony, and violent juxtaposition. (Hlynka, 1991, p. 28).

Practice Theoretical and experiential knowledge to the solution of problems.

Print Technologies Are ways to produce or deliver materials, such as books and static visual materials, primarily through mechanical or photographic printing processes.

Problem Analysis Involves determining the nature and parameters of the problem by using information-gathering and decision-making strategies.

Procedural Models Models which describe how to perform a task . . . [they are] prescriptive, and can serve as guides to the solution of specific problems (Richey, 1986, p. 17, 19).

Process A series of operations or activities directed toward a particular result.

Processing Consists of changing some aspect of information to make it more suitable for some purpose (Lindenmayer, 1988, p. 317).

Program Evaluation Assessing educational activities which provide services on a continuing basis and often involve curricular offerings (Joint Committee on Standards for Educational Evaluation, 1981, p. 12).

Programmed Instruction A method of presenting instructional material printed in small bits or frames, each of which includes an item of information (prompt), an incomplete sentence to be completed or a question to be answered (response), and the correct answer (reinforcement) (Heinich, Molenda and Russell, 1993, p. 447).

Program A set of instructions describing actions for a computer to perform in order to accomplish some task; while conforming to the rules and conventions of a particular programming language (Unwin and McAleese, 1988, p. 450).

Programming Planning a program for a computer or telecommunications medium.

Project Evaluation Evaluation that assesses activities that are funded for a defined period of time to perform a specific task (Joint Committee on Standards for Educational Evaluation, 1981, pp. 12,13).

Project Management Involves planning, monitoring and controlling instructional design and development projects.

Provider Someone who is attempting to convince others to use an innovation.

Qualitative Research An approach to scientific inquiry which typically uses non-experimental methods, such as ethnography or case history, to study important variables that are not easily manipulated or controlled and which emphasizes using multiple methods for collecting, recording and analyzing data rather than statistical analysis.

Quantitative Research An approach to scientific inquiry that typically manipulates independent variables in controlled conditions using experimental designs that incorporate statistical methods of data analysis.

Regulations See Policies and Regulations.

Research Scholarly or scientific investigation or inquiry.

Resources Sources of support for learning, including support systems and instructional materials and environments.

Resource Management Involves planning, monitoring, and controlling resource support systems and services.

Screen Design Planning images on computer screens, both text and visual, that adhere to principles of message design and aesthetics. See Text Design.

Situated Learning [An instructional strategy requiring that] students work on authentic tasks whose execution takes place in a "real world" setting (Winn, 1993, p. 16).

Specifications Explicit and detailed statements about design requirements.

Static Visuals Visual images which are perceived as a still picture or representation.

Structured Writing Properties, i. e. blocks, of the text, especially organization and structure, that permit the structure of the subject matter and the document to be perceived by the reader (Horn, 1982, pp. 242 and 243).

Systematic Using processes or step-by-step procedures that allow one to create systems composed of interrelated, interworking elements that together constitute a whole.

Systemic Design Concurrent and creative consideration of the many aspects of a situation which can affect the learning process (Richey, 1992, p. 9).

Summative Evaluation Involves gathering information on adequacy and using this information to make decisions about utilization.

Task Analysis A process used to determine how a task is performed and to identify the attributes that affect performance (Wolfe, Wetzel, Harris, Mazour and Riplinger, 1991, p. 170).

Technology Systematized practical knowledge which improves productivity.

Theory Concepts, constructs, principles and propositions that contribute to the body of knowledge.

Text Design Applying principles for sequencing, structuring, designing, and laying-out the printed page, whether that text is reproduced on paper or on a computer screen, in order to more effectively present written discourse (Jonassen, 1982, p. ix).

Usage Simple, spontaneous or planned, one time use of an instructional material or technique.

User Someone who is a potential adopter of the innovation.

Utilization Is the act of using processes and resources for learning.

Visual Communication Using visual symbols to express ideas or convey meaning (Seels, 1993d).

Visual Language Non-verbal languages such as sign language, body language, pictographic languages or the elements of visual communication such as shots and composition.

Visual Learning Learning from visuals or research on designing visuals for instruction (Seels, 1993d).

Visual Literacy The ability to understand and use images, including the ability to think, learn and express oneself in terms of images (Bradin and Hortin, 1982, p. 41).

Visual Thinking Organizing mental images around shapes, lines, colors, textures and compositions (Wileman, 1980, p. 13).

Appendices

Appendix A

Some Sources for Glossaries of Instructional Technology

Appendix B

Instructional Technology Associations and Journals

Appendix C

AECT Code of Ethics

APPENDIX A

Some Sources for Glossaries of Instructional Technology

Appendix A presents the same list organized two ways, by subject and alphabetically. These lists include two types of sources:

- books and monographs that are entirely devoted to presenting a glossary, and

- books and articles that include a glossary with other text material.

Books and monographs that present *only* a glossary are indicated by an asterisk (*) after the citation.

Part I
Subject List of Glossary Sources

General Glossaries

Anglin, G. (Ed.). (1991). *Instructional technology: Past, present, and future*. Englewood, CO: Libraries Unlimited.

Ellington, H. and Harris, D. (1986). *Dictionary of instructional technology*. New York: Nichols Publishing.*

Ely, D. P. (1992). *Trends in educational technology*. Syracuse, NY: ERIC Clearinghouse on Information Resources.

Ely, D. P. (Ed.). (1963). The changing role of the audiovisual process in education: A definition and glossary of related terms. *AV Communication Review, 11*(Supplement 6), 1–148.*

Hylnka, D. and Belland, J. C. (Eds.). (1991). *Paradigms regained: The uses of illuminative, semiotic, and post-modern criticism as modes of inquiry in educational technology, a book of readings*. Englewood Cliffs, NJ: Educational Technology Publications.

Seels, B.B. and Richey, R.C. (1994). *Instructional technology: The definition and domains of the field*. Washington, DC: Association for Educational Communications and Technology.

Silber, K. (Ed.). (1979). *Educational technology: A glossary of terms*. Washington, D.C.: Association for Educational Communications and Technology.*

Unwin, D. and McAleese, R. (1988). *The encyclopaedia of educational media communications and technology*. New York: Greenwood Press.*

Foreign Language Glossaries

Glossary of educational technology terms. (1992). Paris: UNIPUB, UNESCO.* Available in English and German.

Glossary of educational technology terms. (1987). Paris: UNIPUB, UNESCO.* Available in English and French.

Glossary of educational technology terms. (1986). Paris: UNIPUB, UNESCO.* Available in English and Russian and English and Spanish.

UNESCO. (1984). *Glossary of educational technology terms*. NY: French and European Publications.* Available in French and English.

Walker, W. G. (1973). *Glossary of educational terms: Usage in five English-Speaking countries*. St. Lucia, Queensland: University of Queensland Pr.*

Design Domain Glossaries

Briggs, L. (1977). *Instructional design: Principles and applications*. Englewood Cliffs, NJ: Educational Technology Publications.

Dick, W. and Carey, L. (1990). *Systematic design of instruction*. (3rd Ed.) New York: Harper Collins.

Dick, W. and Reiser, R. A. (1989). *Planning effective instruction*. Englewood Cliffs, NJ: Prentice Hall.

Gentry, C.G. (1994). *Introduction to Instructional Development*. Belmont, CA: Wadsworth Publishing.

Hlynka, D. (1994). Glossary of terms. *Educational Technology, 34*(2), 14–15.

Sonnier, I. L. (1989). *Affective education: Methods and techniques.* Englewood Cliffs, NJ: Educational Technology Publications.

Wolfe, P., Wetzel, M., Harris, G., Mazour, T. and Riplinger, J. (1991). *Job task analysis: Guide to good practice.* Englewood Cliffs, NJ: Educational Technology Publications.

Development Domain Glossaries

Darcy, L. and Boston, L. (1983). *Webster's new world dictionary of computer terms.* New York: Simon and Schuster.*

Gallini, J. K. and Gredler, M. E. (1989). *Instructional design for computers.* Glenview, IL: Scott Foresman.

Gross, L. S. (1986). *The new television technologies.* Dubuque, IA: William C. Brown.

Guide to audiovisual terminology (Product information supplement #6). (1968). *The EPIE Forum.* New York: Educational Products Information Exchange.*

Kemp, J. and Dayton, D. K. (1985). *Planning and producing educational media.* New York: Harper and Row.

Lochte, R. H. (1993). *Interactive television and instruction.* Englewood Cliffs, NJ: Educational Technology Publications.

Lockard, J., Abrams, P. D. and Many, W. A. (1987). *Microcomputers for educators.* Boston: Little Brown.

Miller, R. L.; Syers, J.; Reeve, V. & Kaston, A. (1991). *Multimedia and related technologies: A glossary of terms.* Falls Church, VA: Future Systems, Inc.*

Schwier, R. (1987). *Interactive video.* Englewood Cliffs, NJ: Educational Technology Publications.

Schwier, R. A. and Misanchuk, E. R. (1993). *Interactive multimedia instruction.* Englewood Cliffs, NJ: Educational Technology Publications.

Shelly, G. B. and Cashman, T. J. (1980). *Introduction to computers and data processing*. Brea, CA: Anaheim Publishing.

Simonson, M. R. and Volker, R. P. (1984). *Media planning and production*. Columbus, OH: Charles E. Merrill.

Venezky, R. and Osin, L. (1991). *The intelligent design of computer-assisted instruction*. NY: Longman.

Wileman, R. E. (1993). *Visual communicating*. Englewood Cliffs, NJ: Educational Technology Publications.

Willis, B. (1993). *Distance education: A Practical Guide*. Englewood Cliffs, NJ: Educational Technology Publications.

Utilization Domain Glossaries

Heinich, R., Molenda, M. and Russell, J. (1993). *Instructional media and the new technologies*. New York: Macmillan Publishing Company.

Management Domain Glossaries

Rosenberg, K. C. and Elsbree, J. J. (1989). *Dictionary of library and educational technology*. Englewood, CO: Libraries Unlimited.*

Evaluation Domain Glossaries

Kaufman, R. (1986). A Glossary of Planning and Organizational Improvement Terms. In *An Introduction to Performance Technology Volume 1*. (pp. 52–56). Washington, DC: National Society for Performance and Instruction.

Kaufman, R. and English, F. (1979). *Needs Assessment: Concept and Application*. Englewood Cliffs, NJ: Educational Technology Publications

Part II
Alphabetical List of Glossary Sources

Anglin, G. (Ed.). (1991). *Instructional technology: Past, present, and future*. Englewood, CO: Libraries Unlimited.

Briggs, L. (1977). *Instructional design: Principles and applications*. Englewood Cliffs, NJ: Educational Technology Publications.

Darcy, L. and Boston, L. (1983). *Webster's new world dictionary of computer terms*. NY: Simon and Schuster.*

Dick, W. and Carey, L. (1990). *Systematic design of instruction*. (3rd. Ed.) New York: Harper Collins.

Dick, W. and Reiser, R. A. (1989). *Planning effective instruction*. Englewood Cliffs, NJ: Prentice Hall.

Ellington, H. and Harris, D. (1986). *Dictionary of instructional technology*. New York: Nichols Publishing.*

Ely, D. P. (Ed.). (1963). The changing role of the audiovisual process in education: A definition and glossary of related terms. *AV Communication Review*, *11* (Supplement 6), 1–148.*

Ely, D. P. (1992). *Trends in educational technology*. Syracus, NY: ERIC Clearinghouse on Information Resources.

Glossary of educational technology terms. (1986). Paris: UNIPUB, UNESCO.* Available in English and Russian and English and Spanish.

Glossary of educational technology terms. (1987). Paris: UNIPUB, UNESCO.* Available in English and French.

Glossary of educational technology terms. (1992). Paris: UNIPUB, UNESCO.* Available in English and German.

Gallini, J. K. and Gredler, M. E. (1989). *Instructional design for computers*. Glenview, IL: Scott Foresman.

Gentry, C.G. (1994). *Introduction to instructional development*. Belmont, CA: Wadsworth Publishing.

Gross, L. S. (1986). *The new television technologies*. Dubuque, IA: William C. Brown.

Guide to audiovisual terminology (Product information supplement #6). (1968). *The EPIE Forum*. NY: Educational Products Information Exchange.*

Heinich, R., Molenda, M. and Russell, J. (1993). *Instructional media and the new technologies.* New York: Macmillan Publishing Company.

Hlynka, D. (1994). Glossary of terms. *Educational Technology, 34*(2), 14–15.

Hylnka, D. and Belland, J. C. (Eds.). (1991). *Paradigms regained: The uses of illuminative, semiotic, and post-modern criticism as modes of inquiry.in educational technology, a book of readings.* Englewood Cliffs, NJ: Educational Technology Publications.

Kemp, J. and Dayton, D. K. (1985). *Planning and producing educational media.* New York: Harper and Row.

Kaufman, R. (1986). A Glossary of Planning and Organizational Improvement Terms.

In *An Introduction to Performance Technology Volume 1.* (pp. 52–56). Washington, DC: National Society for Performance and Instruction.

Kaufman, R. and English, F. (1979). *Needs Assessment: Concept and Application.* Englewood Cliffs, NJ: Educational Technology Publications.

Lochte, R. H. (1993). *Interactive television and instruction.* Englewood Cliffs, NJ: Educational Technology Publications.

Lockard, J.; Abrams, P. D. & Many, W. A. (1987). *Microcomputers for educators.* Boston: Little Brown.

Miller, R. L.; Syers, J.; Reeve, V. & Kaston, A. (1991). *Multimedia and related technologies: A glossary of terms.* Falls Church, VA: Future Systems, Inc.

Rosenberg, K. C. and Elsbree, J. J. (1989). *Dictionary of library and educational technology.* Englewood, CO: Libraries Unlimited.*

Schwier, R. (1987). *Interactive video.* Englewood Cliffs, NJ: Educational Technology Publications.

Schwier, R. A. and Misanchuk, E. R. (1993). *Interactive multimedia instruction.* Englewood Cliffs, NJ: Educational Technology Publications.

Seels, B.A. and Richey, R. C. (1994). *Instructional technology: The definition and domains of the field*. Washington, D.C.: Association for Educational Communications and Technology.

Siebert, I. N., project officer. (1975). *A handbook of standard terminology and a guide for recording and reporting information about educational technololgy*. Washington, DC: National Center for Educational Statistics. (NCES 76–321).

Silber, K. (Ed.). (1979). *Educational technology: A glossary of terms*. Washington, DC: Association for Educational Communications and Technology.*

Simonson, M. R. and Volker, R. P. (1984). *Media planning and production*. Columbus, OH: Charles E. Merrill.

Shelly, G. B. and Cashman, T. J. (1980). *Introduction to computers and data processing*. Brea, CA: Anaheim Publishing.

Sonnier, I. L. (1989). *Affective education: Methods and techniques*. Englewood Cliffs, NJ: Educational Technology Publications.

UNESCO. (1984). *Glossary of educational technology terms*. NY: French and European Publications.* Available in French and English.

Unwin, D. and McAleese, R. (1988). *The encyclopaedia of educational media communications and technology*. New York: Greenwood Press.*

Venezky, R. and Osin, L. (1991). *The intelligent design of computer-assisted instruction*. NY: Longman.

Walker, W. G. (1973). *Glossary of educational terms: Usage in five English-speaking countries*. St. Lucia, Queensland: University of Queensland Pr.*

Wileman, R. E. (1993). *Visual communicating*. Englewood Cliffs, NJ: Educational Technology Publications.

Willis, B. (1993). *Distance education: A practical guide*. Englewood Cliffs, NJ: Educational Technology Publications.

Wolfe, P.; Wetzel, M.; Harris, G., Mazour, T. and Riplinger, J. (1991). *Job task analysis: Guide to good practice*. Englewood Cliffs, NJ: Educational Technology Publications.

APPENDIX B

Instructional Technology Associations, Journals, and Newsletters and Organizations: A Partial Listing

Appendix B has three parts:

Part I. Associations and Their Publications

Part II. Journals from Other Sources

Part III. Other Organizations

The most complete source of information on associations, organizations and publications in the field in the *Educational Media andTechnology Yearbook* published annually by Libraries Unlimited in cooperation with the ERIC Clearinghouse on Information Resources and AECT. Although the content of the yearbook changes from year to year, it usually includes: 1) a directory and index to producers, distributors and publishers; 2) addresses of graduate programs in the field; and 3) addresses of organizations and associations in North America.

Readers who wish a more extensive list can use electronic mail to access a listing of Educational Technology Professional Resources submitted by readers of EDTECH@OHSTVMA.BITNET. This electronic mail list includes juried and trade publications, professional associations and networks, service organizations, and grant sources. It is kept up-to-date through skulikow@UWF.bitnet.

In addition, readers who need more information on organizations and publications related to computer-based technologies are referred to:

Bitter, G., Camuse, R. A. and Durbin, V. L. (1993). *Using a microcomputer in the classroom.* Boston: Allyn and Bacon.

This book includes lists of "Educational Computing Magazines and Newsletters," "Microcomputer Magazines," "Software Directories," and "Software Resources".

Venezky, R. and Osin, L. (1991) *The intelligent design of instruction.* New York: Longman Publishing Group.

This book includes a "Compendium of Organizations in the Field of CAI".

Part I
Associations and Their Publications

American Association for Adult and Continuing Education
2101 Wilson Boulevard, Ste. 925, Arlington, VA 22201
tel. (703) 522-2234
Publishes: *Adult Education Quarterly*

American Educational Research Association (AERA)
1230 17th Street, NW, Washington, DC 20036
tel. (202) 223-9485
Publishes: *American Educational Research Journal Educational Researcher*

American Library Association (ALA)
American Association for School Librarians
50 East Huron Street, Chicago, IL 60611
tel. (312) 944-6780
Publishes: *School Library Media Quarterly*

American Psychological Association (APA)
750 1st St., NE, Washington, DC 20002-4242
tel. (202) 336-5500
Publishes: *American Psychologist Journal of Educational Psychology*

American Society for Training and Development (ASTD)
P.O. Box 1443, 1640 King Street, Alexandria, VA 22313
tel. (703) 683-8100
Publishes: *Training and Development Journal*

Association for the Advancement of Computing in Education
P.O. Box 2966, Charlottesville, VA 22902-2966
tel. (804) 973-3987
Publishes: *Journal of Artifical Intelligence in Education Journal of Educational Multimedia & Hypermedia Journal of Technology and Teacher Education*

Association for Business and Experimental Learning
Sage Publications, Inc.
2455 Teller Road, Newbury Park, CA 91320
tel. (805) 499-0721
Publishes: *Simulations and Gaming*

Association for the Development of Computer-Based Instructional
Systems (ADCIS)
1601 W. 5th. Ave., Ste 111, Columbus, OH 43212
tel. (614) 487-1528
Publishes: *Journal of Computer Based Instruction*

Association for Educational Communications and Technology (AECT)
1025 Vermont Ave., NW, Suite 820, Washington, DC 20005
tel. (202) 347-7834
Publishes: *Tech Trends; Educational Technology Research and
Development*

Association for Educational and Training Technology (AETT)
c/o The City University Centre for Continuing Education
Northhampton Sq., London ECIV OHB, England
tel. 71 253-4399
Publishes: *Programmed Learning & Educational Technology; Educational
Training and Technology International*

Association for Media and Technology in Education in Canada
3-1750 The Queensway, Suite 1318, Etobicoke, Ontario M9C 58H
Canada
Publishes: *Canadian Journal of Educational Communication*

Association for Multi-Image International Inc.
10008 N. Dale Mabry, Suite 113, Tampa, FL 33618
tel. (813) 960-1692
Publishes: *Multi-Images Journal*

Association of Special Education Technology
Box 328, Peabody College, Nashville, TN 37203
tel. (615) 322-8165
Publishes: *Journal of Special Education Technology*

Association for Technology in Music Instruction (ATMI)
c/o Gary Karpinski, President ATMI
Department of Music and Dance, University of Massachusetts
Amherst, MA 01003
tel. (413) 545-4229
Publishes: *ATMI International Newsletter; ATMI Technology Directory*

Australian Society for Educational Technology (ASET)
P.O. Box 772, Bel connen, A.C.T. 2616, Australia
tel. 616-259-1980
Publishes: *Australian Journal of Educational Technology*

Council for Educational Technology for the United Kingdom
3 Devonshire Street, London W1N 2BA, England
tel. 01 636-4186
Publishes: *British Journal of Educational Technology*

Educational Television Association (ETA)
The King's Manor, Exhibition Square
York, N. Yorkshire, Y01 2EP, England
tel. 904-433-929
Publishes: *Journal of Educational Television*

Educational Technology Journal Association of Japan
Japan Scientific Societies Press
6-2-10 Hongo, Bunkyo-ku, Tokyo 113, Japan
tel. 3814-2001
Publishes: *Japan Journal of Educational Technology*

Human Factors Society
Box 1369, Santa Monica, CA 90406-1369
tel. (301) 394-1811
Publishes: *Human Factors*

International Association for Learning Laboratories (IALL)
c/oRobin Lawrason, Media Learning Center, (022-31),
Temple University, Philadelphia, PA 19122
tel. (215) 787-4758
Publishes: *IALL Journal of Language Learning Technologies*

International Communication Industries Association (ICIA)
3150 Spring Street, Fairfax, VA 22031
tel. (703) 273-7200
Publishes: *The Equipment Directory of Video Computer and Audio-Visual Products*

International Council of Educational Media (ICEM)
c/o Robert LeFranc, ICEM Secretariat, 29 rue d'Ulm
75230 Paris, Cedex 05 France
tel. 331 46571117 Ext. 561
Publishes: *Educational Media International*

International Interactive Communications Society (IICS)
Box 1862, Lake Oswego, OR 97035
tel. (503) 649-2035
Publishes: *IICS Reporter; Interact*

International Simulation and Gaming Association (ISAGA)
c/o Steven Underwood, University of Michigan
4117 EECS Building, Ann Arbor, MI 48109-2122
tel. (313) 936-2999
Publishes: *Simulation and Games: An International Journal of Theory, Design and Research*

International Society for Technology in Education (ISTE)
University of Oregon
1787 Agate St., Eugene, OR 97403
tel. (503) 346-4414
Publishes: *Journal of Research on Computing in Education; Computing Teacher*

International Television Association (ITVA)
6311 N. O'Connor Road, LB 51, Irving, TX 75039
tel. (214) 869-1112
Publishes: *Video Systems*

International Visual Literacy Association (IVLA)
Virginia Polytechnical Institute and State University, Educational Technologies-LRC
Blacksburg, VA 24061-0232
tel. (703) 231-8992
Publishes: *Journal of Visual Literacy; Visual Literacy Review*

Japan Audio-Visual Education Association (JAVEA)
Nihon Shichokaku Kyoiku Kyokai, 1-17-1, Toranomon, Minato-Ku, Tokyo 105, Japan
Publishes: *AVE in Japan* (Audio-Visual Education)

Micrcomputer Software and Information for Teachers (Microsoft)
Northwest Regional Educational Laboratory (NREL)
1005 W. Main Street, Suite 500, Portland, OR 97204
tel. (503) 275-9500
Publishes: *Microsoft Software Catalog List*

National Society for Performance and Instruction (NSPI)
1300 L Street, NW, Suite 1250, Washington, DC 20005
tel. (202) 408-7969
Publishes: *Performance and Instruction; Performance Improvement Quarterly*

North American Simulation and Gaming Association (NASAGA)
c/o John Del Regato, Pentathalon Institute
Box 20590, Indianapolis, IN 46220-0590
tel. (317) 782-1553
Publishes: *Handbook of Simulation Gaming*

Society for Applied Learning Technology
50 Culpepper Street, Warrenton, VA 22186
tel. (703) 347-0055
Publishes: *Journal of Interactive Delivery; Instruction Delivery Systems*

Society for the Advancement of Games and Simulation in Education (SAGSET)
Centre for Extension Studies, University of Technology
Loughborough, Leics LE11 3 TU United Kingdom
Publishes: *Simulation/Games for Learning*

Part II
Journals from Other Sources

American Journal of Distance Education
Office for Distance of Education/College of Education, The Pennsylvania State University
403 S. Allen St., Suite 206, University Park, PA 16802-5202
tel. (814) 863-3764

Computers and Education
Pergamon Press, Inc., Journals Division
White Plains Road, Tarrytown, NY 10591-5153
tel. (914) 524-9200

Education and Computing: The International Journal
Elsevier Science Publishing Co.
Box 882, Madison Square Station, New York, NY 10159
tel. (212) 989-5800

Educational Technology: The Magazine for Managers of Change in Education
Educational Technology Publications, Inc.
700 Palisades Avenue, Englewood Cliffs, NJ 07632
tel. (201) 871-4007

Instructional Science: An International Journal
Martinus Nijhoss Publishers, c/o Cluwer Academic Publishers Group
Distribution Center
Box 358, Accord Station, Hingham, MA 0218-0358
tel. (617) 871-6600

Journal of Computer Assisted Learning
Blackwell Scientific Publications, LTD.
Osney Mead, Oxford, OX2 0EL, England
tel. 0865-240201

Journal of Educational Computing Research
Journal of Educational Technology Systems
Baywood Publishing Co.
26 Austin Ave., Box 337, Amityville, NY 11701
tel. (576) 691-1270

Studies in the Education of Adults
National Institute of Adult Continuing Education
19 DeMonfort Street, Leicester LE1 7GE
England
tel. 0533-551451

Technology in Society: An International Journal
Pergamon Press, Inc., Journals Division
White Plains Road, Tarrytown, NY 10591-5153
tel. (914) 524-9200

T.H.E. Journal (Technological Horizons in Education)
150 El Camino Real, Suite 112, Tustin, CA 92680-3670
tel. (714) 730-4011

Training: The Magazine of Human Resources Development
Lakewood Publications, Inc.
50 S. Ninth Street, Minneapolis, MN 55402
tel. (612) 333-0471

*Visual Language: The Quarterly Concerned with All That Is Involved in
Our Being Literate.*
Journal of Typographic Research
Rhode Island School of Design
2 College st., Providence, RI 02903
tel. (401) 331-3571

Part III
Other Organizations

Children's Television Workshop (CTW)
1 Lincoln Plaza, New York, NY 10023

Community College Association
For Instruction & Technology (CCAIT)
(contact AECT for address of current President)

Consortium of College & University
Media Centers (CCUMC)
MRC, Iowa State University
121 Pearson Hall, Ames IA 5011-2203

Educational Products Information Exchange Institute (EPIE)
103-3 W. Montank Highway, Hampton Bays, NY 11946

ERIC Clearinghouse on Information and Technology
4-194 Center for Science & Technology
Syracuse University, Syracuse, NY 13244-4100

Federal Educational Technology Association (FETA)
Applied Science Associates, Inc.
7926 Jones Branch Drive, Suite 600, McLean, VA 22102

Health Sciences Communications Association (HeSCA)
6728 Old McLean Village Dr., McLean, VA 22101

Hypermedia and Instructional Software Clearinghouse
University of Colorado—Denver
Campus Box 906, Denver, CO 80217-3364

Interactive Video Industry Association (IVIA)
1900 L Street NW, Suite 500, Washington, DC 20036

Learning Through Media Coalition
(contact AECT for current mailing address)

Minorities in Media (MIM)
(contact AECT for current mailing address)

National Association of Regional Media Centers (NARMC)
(contact AECT for current mailing address)

National Instructional Television Fixed Service Association
Box #1130, 3421 M Street, NW, Washington, DC 20007

APPENDIX C

AECT Code of Ethics

Preamble

1. The Code of Ethics contained herein shall be considered to be principles of ethics. these principles are intended to aid members individually and collectively in maintaining a high level of professional conduct.
2. The Professional Ethics Committee will build documentation of opinion (interpretive briefs or ramifications of intent) relating to specific ethical statements enumerated herein.
3. Opinions may be generated in response to specific cases brought before the Professional Ethics Committee.
4. Amplification and/or clarification of the ethical principles may be generated by the Committee in response to a request submitted by a member.

Section 1
Commitment to the Individual

In fulfilling obligations to the individual, the members:
1. Shall encourage independent action in an individual's pursuit of learning and shall provide access to varying points of view.
2. Shall protect the individual rights of access to materials of varying points of view.
3. Shall guarantee to each individual the opportunity to participate in any appropriate program.
4. Shall conduct professional business so as to protect the privacy and maintain the personal integrity of the individual.
5. Shall follow sound professional procedures for evaluation and selection of materials and equipment.
6. Shall make reasonable effort to protect the individual from conditions harmful to health and safety.
7. Shall promote current and sound professional practices in the use of technology in education.
8. Shall in the design and selection of any educational program or media seek to avoid content that reinforces or promotes gender, ethnic, racial, or religious stereotypes. Shall seek to encourage the development of programs and media that emphasize the diversity of our society as a multi-cultural community.

Section 2
Commitment to Society

In fulfilling obligations to society, the member:
1. Shall honestly represent the institution or organization with which that person is affiliated, and shall take adequate precautions to distinguish between personal and institutional or organizational views.
2. Shall represent accurately and truthfully the facts concerning educational matters in direct and indirect public expressions.
3. Shall not use institutional or Associational privileges for private gain.
4. Shall accept no gratuities, gifts, or favors that might impair or appear to impair professional judgment, or offer any favor, service, or thing of value to obtain special advantage.
5. Shall engage in fair and equitable practices with those rendering service to the profession.

Section 3
Commitment to the Profession

In fulfilling obligations to the profession, the member:
1. Shall accord just and equitable treatment to all members of the profession in terms of professional rights and responsibilities.
2. Shall not use coercive means to promote special treatment in order to influence professional decisions of colleagues.
3. Shall avoid commercial exploitation of that person's membership in the Association.
4. Shall strive continually to improve professional knowledge and skill and to make available to patrons and colleagues the benefits of that person's professional attainments.
5. Shall present honestly personal professional qualifications and the professional qualifications and evaluations of colleagues.
6. Shall conduct professional business through proper channels.
7. Shall delegate assigned tasks only to qualified personnel. Qualified perennial are those who have appropriate training or credentials and/or who can demonstrate competency in performing the task.
8. Shall inform users of the stipulations and interpretations of the copyright law and other laws affecting the profession and encourage compliance.
9. Shall observe all laws relating to or affecting the profession; shall report, without hesitation, illegal or unethical conduct of fellow members of the profession to the AECT Professional Ethics Committee; shall participate in professional inquiry when requested by the Association.

References

The following list includes all citations used in this book, including the glossary and the appendices. Efforts have been made to have this reference list cover many of the classic pieces of literature in the field of Instructional Technology, as well as many current additions. Thus, to some extent, this list serves as a type of chronology of the field.

Association for Educational Communications and Technology. (1972). The field of educational technology: a statement of definition. *Audio-Visual Instruction, 17(8)*, 36-43.

Anglin, G.J. (Ed.). (1991). *Instructional technology: Past, present, and future.* Englewood, CO: Libraries Unlimited, Inc.

Alessi, S. M., and Trollip, S. R. (1985). *Computer-based instruction: Methods and development.* Englewood Cliffs, NJ: Prentice-Hall.

Armsey, J.W. and Dahl, N.C. (1973). *An inquiry into the uses of instructional technology.* A Ford Foundation Report.

Arnheim, R. (1972). *Visual thinking.* Berkeley, CA: University of California Press.

Association for Educational Communications and Technology. (1975). *A handbook of standard terminology and a guide for recording and reporting information about educational technology.* Washington, D.C.: AECT.

Association for Educational Communications and Technology. (1977). *The definition of educational technology.* Washington, D.C.: AECT.

Bailey, G.D. (1993). Wanted: A road map for understanding integrated learning systems. In G.D. Bailey (Ed.), *Computer-based integrated learning systems* (pp. 3–9). Englewood Cliffs, NJ: Educational Technology Publications.

Baker, E. L. (1972). Using measurement to improve instruction. A paper presented at the Annual Meeting of the American Psychological Association, Honolulu.

Baker, E.L. and O'Neil, H. (1985). *Assessing instructional outcomes* (Contract No. NIE G-83-0001). Los Angeles: Center for the Study of Evaluation, University of California. (ERIC Document Reproduction Service No. ED 266 175).

Barson, J. (1967). *Instructional systems development: A demonstration and evaluation project.* U.S. Office of Education, Title II-B. Project OE 3-16-025, Michigan State University.

Becker, W.E. and Davis, R.W. (1983). An economic model of training in an industrial setting. *Journal of instructional development, 6*(2), 27–32.

Bennis, W.G. (1969). *Organizational development: Its nature, origins, and prospects.* Reading, MA: Addison-Wesley.

Berlo, D.K. (1960). *The process of communication.* New York: Holt, Rinehart & Winston.

Bern, H.A. (1967). Wanted: Educational engineers. *Phi Delta Kappan,* 230–236.

Berry, L. (1992). Visual complexity and pictorial memory: A fifteen year research perspective. A paper presented at the 1992 Annual Meeting of the Association for Educational Communications and Technology at Washington, D.C.

Bloom, B.S. (1956). *Taxonomy of educational objectives, Handbook I: Cognitive domain.* New York: David McKay Company.

Bloom, B.S. (1976). *Human characteristics and school learning.* New York: McGraw Hill Company.

Boothe, B. (1984). Certification—beyond reason. *Performance & Instruction Journal, 23*(1), 19–20.

Bowers, C.A. (1988). *The cultural dimensions of educational computing: Understanding the non-neutrality of technology.* New York: Teachers College Press.

Braden, R.A. (1992). Formative evaluation: A revised descriptive theory and a prescriptive model. In M.R. Simonson and K.A. Jurasek (Eds.), *Proceedings of selected research and development presentations at the 1992 convention of the Association for Educational Communications and Technology* (pp.70–85). ERIC Document Reproduction Service Nos. ED 347 970 to ED 348 041.

Braden, R.A. and Hortin, J.L. (1982). Identifying the theoretical foundations of visual literacy. *Journal of Visual/Verbal Languaging, 2,* 37–42.

Bradford, J.C. (1987). *Ten year follow-up study of the development of a quarter plan to provide year-round schools in grades 9–12 in the city of Buena Vista.* Buena Vista, CA: Buena Vista City Public Schools. (ERIC Document Reproduction Service No. ED 303 908).

Branyan-Broadbent, B. and Wood, R. K. (Eds.). (1993). *Educational media and technology yearbook.* Englewood, CO: Libraries Unlimited.

Braudel, F. (1979). *The structures of everyday life: The limits of the possible, Vol.1.* New York: Harper and Row.

Briggs, L.J. (1968). *Sequencing of instruction in relation to hierarchies of competence.* Pittsburgh: American Institutes for Research.

Briggs, L. (1977). *Instructional design: Principles and applications.* Englewood Cliffs, NJ: Educational Technology Publications.

Briggs, L.J.; Campeau, P.L.; Gagné, R.M.; and May, M.A. (1967). *Instructional media: A procedure for the design of multi-media instruction, a critical review of research, and suggestions for future research.* Pittsburgh: American Institutes for Research.

Briggs, L.; Gustafson, K.; and Tillman, M. H. (Eds.) (1991). *Instructional design principles and applications* (2nd Ed.). Englewood Cliffs, NJ: Educational Technology Publications.

Brinkerhoff, R.O.; Brethower,D.M.; Hluchyj, T.; and Nowakowski, J.R. (1983). *Program evaluation: A practitioner's guide for trainers and educators.* Boston: Kluwer-Nijhoff.

Brooks, H. (1980). Technology, evolution and purpose. *Daedalus: Journal of the American Academy of Arts & Sciences, 109*(1), 65–82.

Brown, J.S. and Duguid, P. (1993). Stolen knowledge. *Educational Technology, 33*(3), 10–15.

Bruner, J.S. (1966). *Toward a theory of instruction.* Cambridge, MA: The Belknap Press of Harvard University Press.

Burgoon, M. and Ruffner, M. (1978). *Human communication* (2nd Ed.). New York: Holt, Rinehart and Winston.

Burkman, E. (1987). Factors affecting utilization. In R. M. Gagné (Ed.). *Instructional Technology: Foundations* (pp. 429–456). Hillsdale, NJ: Lawrence Erlbaum Associates.

Burns, H.W. (1964). An axiological dimension of systems analysis in education. A paper presented at the Conference on New Dimensions for Research in Educational Media Implied by the Systems Approach to Education, Syracuse University.

Caffarella, E.P. (1993). The knowledge base of the management domain. A paper presented at the 1993 Annual Meeting of the Association for Educational Communications and Technology at New Orleans, LA.

Caffarella, E.P. (1991). *Doctoral research in instructional design and technology: A directory of dissertations 1987–1988.* Washington, D.C.: Association for Educational Communications and Technology.

Caffarella, E.P. and Sachs, S.G. (1988). *Doctoral research in instructional design and technology: A directory of dissertations 1977–1986.* Washington, D.C.: Association for Educational Communications and Technology.

Caffarella, E.P.; Earle, R.S.; Hanclosky, W.; and Richey, R.C. (1994). Guidelines for the accreditation of programs in educational communication and information technologies. (3rd Ed.) Washington, D.C.: Association for Educational Communications and Technology.

Canning, T. and Finkel, L. (1993). *The technology age in the classroom.* Wilsonville, OR: Franklin, Beedle & Associates.

Carpenter, C.R. and Greenhill, L.P. (1956). *Instructional film reports, Vol. 2.* Technical report 269-7-61. Port Washington, NY: Special Devices Center, U.S. Navy.

Carrier, C. and Sales, G. (1987). A taxonomy for the design of computer-based instruction. *Educational Technology, 27*(10), 15–17.

Charters, W.W. (1945). Is there a field of educational engineering? *Educational Research Bulletin, 24*(2), 29–37,53.

Chisholm, M.E. and Ely, D.P. (1976). *Media personnel in education: A competency approach.* Englewood Cliffs, NJ: Prentice-Hall, Inc.

Clark, R. E. (1983). Reconsidering research on learning from media. *Review of Educational Research, 53*, 445–460.

Clark, R. E. (1989). Current progress and future directions for research in instructional technology. *Educational Technology Research and Development, 37*(1), 57–66.

Cleary, A. et al. (1976). *Educational technology: Implications for early and special education.* New York: John Wiley & Sons.

Cobb, R.W. and Elder, C.D. (1983). *Participation in American politics: The dynamics of agenda-building.* (2nd Ed.). Baltimore, MD: The Johns Hopkins University Press.

Cognition and Technology Group at Vanderbilt. (1990). Anchored instruction and its relationship to situated cognition. *Educational Researcher, 19*(6), 2–10.

Cognition and Technology Group at Vanderbilt. (1992). An anchored instruction approach to cognitive skills acquisition and intelligent tutoring. In J.W. Regian and V.J. Shute (Eds.), *Cognitive approaches to automated instruction* (pp. 135–170). Hillsdale, NJ: Lawrence Earlbaum Associates, Publishers.

Commission on Instructional Technology. (1970). *To improve learning: A report to the President and the Congress of the United States.* Washington, D.C.: U.S. Government Printing Office.

Coscarelli, W. (1984). Arguments for certification. *Performance and Instruction Journal, 23*(1), 21–22.

Couch, J.D. and Peterson, A.J. (1991). Multimedia curriculum development: A K–12 campus prepares for the future. *T.H.E. Journal.*

Cuban, L. (1986). *Teachers and machines.* New York: Teachers College Press.

Cunningham, W.G. (1982). *Systematic planning for educational change.* Mountain View, CA: Mayfield Publishing Company.

Curtiss, D. (1987). *An introduction to visual literacy.* Englewood Cliffs, NJ: Prentice Hall.

Dale, E. (1946). *Audio-visual methods in teaching.* New York: Dryden Press.

Darcy, L. and Boston, L. (1983). *Webster's new world dictionary of computer terms.* New York: Simon and Schuster.

Dewey, J. (1916). *Democracy and education.* New York: Macmillan Company.

Dick, W. (1993). Enhanced ISD: A response to changing environments for learning and performance. *Educational Technology, 33*(2), 12–16.

Dick, W. and Carey, L. (1990) *The systematic design of instruction.* (3rd. Ed.). Glenview, IL: Scott, Foresman.

Dick, W. and Reiser, R. A. (1989). *Planning effective instruction.* Englewood Cliffs, NJ: Prentice Hall.

Dieuzeide, H. (1971). *Educational technology: Sophisticated, adapted, and rational technology. Series B: Opinions.* (No. 30) Paris: International Commission on Development of Education, UNESCO.

Dondis, D.A. (1973). *A primer of visual literacy.* Cambridge, MA: MIT Press.

Doughty, P. (1988). Syllabus for cost effectiveness and benchmarking. Summer Institute, June 22–25, 1988, Syracuse University. Unpublished manuscript.

Driscoll, M. P. (1984). Alternative paradigms for research in instructional systems. *Journal of Instructional Development, 7*(4), 2–5.

Duchastel, P.C. (1987). Structures and methodologies for the evolution of software. *Studies in Educational Evaluation, 13*, 111–117.

Duffy, T.M. and Jonassen, D.H. (Eds.). (1992). *Constructivism and the technology of instruction: A conversation.* Hillsdale, NJ: Lawrence Erlbaum Associates, Publishers.

Duffy, T.M. and Jonassen, D.H. (1991). Constructivism: New implications for instructional technology? *Educational Technology, 31*(5), 7–12.

Dunn, W.; Holzner, B.; and Zaltman, G. (1989). Knowledge utilization. In M. Eraut (Ed.), *The international encyclopedia of educational technology* (pp. 575–582). Oxford: Pergamon Press.

Dwyer, F.M. (1972). *A guide for improving visualized instruction.* State College, PA: Learning Services.

Dwyer, F.M. (1978). *Strategies for improving visual learning.* State College, PA: Learning Services.

Eastmond, N. (1991). Educational evaluation: The future. *Theory into Practice,* 30(1), 74–79.

Educational media and technology yearbook, Educational Media and Technology: The Year in Review. (An annual section.) Englewood, CO: Libraries Unlimited, Inc. and ERIC Clearinghouse on Information Resources and the Association for Educational Commmunications and Technology.

Eisenberg, M.B. (1991). *Trends and issues in library and information science.* Syracuse, NY: ERIC Clearinghouse on Information Resources, Syracuse University. (Published bi-annually.)

Ellington, H. and Harris, D. (1986). *Dictionary of instructional technology.* London: Kogan Page.

Ely, D.P. (Ed.). (1963). *The changing role of the audiovisual process in education: A definition and a glossary of related terms.* TCP Monograph No. 1. *AV Communication Review, 11*(1), Supplement No.6.

Ely, D.P. (1970). Toward a philosophy of instructional technology. *British Journal of Educational Technology, 1*(2), 81–94.

Ely, D.P. (1972). The field of educational technology: A statement of definition. *Audiovisual Instruction, 17*(8), 36–43.

Ely, D.P. (1973). Defining the field of educational technology. *Audiovisual Instruction, 8*(3), 52–53.

Ely, D.P. (1983). The definition of educational technology: An emerging stability. *Educational Considerations, 10*(2), 2–4.

Ely, D.P. (1992). *Trends in educational technology.* Syracuse, NY: ERIC Clearinghouse on Information Resources.

Ely, D.P. and Minor, B.B. (1992). *Educational media and technology yearbook.* Englewood, CO: Libraries Unlimited, Inc. in cooperation with ERIC Clearinghouse on Information Resources and the Association for Educational Communications and Technology.

Eraut, M. (Ed.). (1989). *The international encyclopedia of educational technology.* NY: Pergamon Press.

Eraut, M. R. (1989). Conceptual frameworks and historical development. In M. Eraut (Ed.), *The International Encyclopedia of Educational Technology* (pp. 11–21). Oxford: Pergamon Press.

Faris, G. (1968). Would you believe . . . an instructional developer? *Audiovisual Instruction,* 13(9), 971–973.

Finn, J. (1953). Professionalizing the audio-visual field. *Audio-visual Communication Review, 1*(1), 6–17.

Finn, J. (1956). AV development and the concept of systems. *Teaching Tools, 3*(4). 163– 164.

Finn, J. (1960). A new theory for instructional technology. *Audio-visual Communications Review, 8,* 84–94.

Finn, J. (1965). Instructional technology. *Audiovisual Instruction, 10*(3), 192–194.

Flagg, B. N. (1990). *Formative evaluation for educational technologies.* Hillsdale, NJ: Lawrence Erlbaum Associates, Publishers.

Fleishman, E.A. and Quaintance, M.K. (1984). *Taxonomies of human performance: The description of human tasks.* Orlando: Academic Press.

Fleming, M. L. (1987). Displays and communication. In R.M. Gagné
(Ed.), *Instructional technology: Foundations* (pp. 233–260).
Hillsdale, NJ: Lawrence Erlbaum Associates.

Fleming, M. and Levie, W.H. (Eds.). (1993). *Instructional message
design: Principles from the behavioral sciences.* (2nd Ed.). Englewood
Cliffs, NJ: Educational Technology Publications, Inc.

Fleming, M. and Levie, W.H. (1978). *Instructional message design:
Principles from the behavioral sciences.* Englewood Cliffs, NJ:
Educational Technology Publications, Inc.

Gage, N. L. (1963). Paradigms for research on teaching. In N. L. Gage
(Ed.), *Handbook of research on teaching* (pp. 94–141). Chicago:
Rand McNally and Company.

Gagné, R.M. (1965). *The conditions of learning.* New York: Holt,
Rinehart and Winston.

Gagné, R.M. (1985). *The conditions of learning and theory of instruction*
(4th Ed.). New York: Holt, Rinehart and Winston.

Gagné, R.M. (Ed.). (1987). *Instructional technology: Foundations.*
Hillsdale, NJ: Lawrence Erlbaum Associates, Publishers.

Gagné, R.M. (1989). *Studies of learning: 50 years of research.*
Tallahassee, FA: Florida State University Learning Systems Institute.

Gagné, R.M. and Briggs, L.J. (1974). *Principles of instructional design.*
New York: Holt Rinehart and Winston.

Gagné, R.M.; Briggs, L.J.; and Wager, W.W. (1992). *Principles of
instructional design* (4th Ed.). Fort Worth, TX: Harcourt Brace
Jovanovich, Publishers.

Gagné, R.M. and Driscoll, M. P. (1988). *Essentials of learning for
instruction* (2nd Ed.). Englewood Cliffs, NJ: Prentice Hall.

Gallini, J. K. and Gredler, M. E. (1989). *Instructional design for
computers.* Glenview, IL: Scott Foresman.

Geis, G. L. (1986). Human performance technology: An overview. In
M.E. Smith (Ed.), *Introduction to performance technology.* Vol 1.
Washington, D.C.: National Society for Performance and Instruction.

Gentry, C.G. (1994). *Introduction to instructional development*. Belmont, CA: Wadsworth Publishing.

Gentry, C. (1991). Educational technology: A question of meaning. In G.J. Anglin (Ed.), *Instructional technology: Past, present, and future* (pp. 1–10). Englewood CO: Libraries Unlimited, Inc.

Gery, G. (1991). *Electronic performance support systems*. Boston, MA: Weingarten Publishers.

Glaser, R. (1965). *Teaching machines and programmed learning, II: Data and directions*. Washington, D.C.: National Education Association of the U.S.

Glaser, R. (1976). Components of a psychology of instruction: Toward a science of design. *Review of Educational Research, 46*(1), 1–24.

Glossary of educational technology terms. (1992). Paris: UNIPUB, UNESCO. Available in English and German.

Glossary of educational technology terms. (1987). Paris: UNIPUB, UNESCO. Available in English and French.

Glossary of educational technology terms. (1986). Paris: UNIPUB, UNESCO. Available in English and Russian and English and Spanish.

Grabowski, B.L. (1991). Message design: Issues and trends. In G.J. Anglin (Ed.), *Instructional technology: Past, present, and future* (pp. 202–212) Englewood, CO: Libraries Unlimited, Inc.

Greer, M. (1992). *ID project management: Tools and techniques for instructional designers and developers*. Englewood Cliffs, NJ: Educational Technology Publications.

Gropper, G. (1991). *Text displays*. Englewood Cliffs, NJ: Educational Technology Publications.

Gross, L. S. (1986). *The new television technologies*. Dubuque, IA: William C. Brown.

Guide to audiovisual terminology (Product information supplement #6). (1968). *The EPIE Forum*. New York: Educational Products Information Exchange.

Gustafson, K. L. (1993). Clouds on the horizon. *Educational Technology*, *33*(2), 27–32.

Gustafson, K. and Bratton, B. (1984). Instructional improvement centers in higher education: A status report. *Journal of Instructional Development*, *7*(2), 2–7.

Gustafson, K.L. and Reeves, T.C. (1990). IDioM: A platform for a course development expert system. *Educational Technology*, *30*(3), 19–25.

Hannafin, M.J. (1992). Emerging technologies, ISD, and learning environments: Critical perspectives. *Educational Technology Research and Development*, *40*(1), 49–63.

Hannum, W. and Hansen, C. (1989). *Instructional systems development in large organizations*. Englewood Cliffs, NJ: Educational Technology Publications.

Harrow, A.J. (1972). *A taxonomy of the pschomotor domain*. New York: David McKay Company.

Havelock, R.G. (1971). The utilization of educational research and development. *British Journal of Educational Technology*, *2*, 84–98.

Heidt, E.U. (1988). Media classification. In D. Unwin and R. McAleese (Eds.), *The encyclopaedia of educational media communications and technology* (2nd. Ed.) (pp. 367–380). New York: Greenwood Press.

Heinich, R. (1984). The proper study of instructional technology. *Educational Communications and Technology Journal*, *32*(2), 67–87.

Heinich, R. (1991). Restructuring, technology, and instructional productivity. In G.J. Anglin (Ed.), *Instructional technology: Past, present, and future*. (pp. 236–240). Englewood CO: Libraries Unlimited.

Heinich, R.; Molenda, M.; and Russell, J.D. (1993). *Instructional media and the new technologies of instruction* (4th Ed.). New York: Macmillan Publishing Company.

Hellebrandt, J. and Russell, J.D. (1993). Confirmative evaluation of instructional materials and learners. *Performance and Instruction*, *32*(6), 22–27.

Henderson, J.M. and Quandt, R.E. (1980). *Microeconomic theory: A mathematical approach* (3rd Ed.). New York: McGraw Hill.

Hlynka, D. (1994). Glossary of terms. *Educational Technology, 34*(2), 14–15.

Hlynka, D. (1991). Postmodern excursions into educational technology. *Educational Technology, 31*(6), 27–30.

Hlynka, D. and Belland, J. (Eds.). (1991). *Paradigms regained: The uses of illuminative, semiotic and post-modern criticism as modes of inquiry in educational technology.* Englewood Cliffs, NJ: Educational Technology Publications.

Hoban, C.F.; Hoban, F.H.; and Zisman, S.B. (1937). *Visualizing the curriculum.* New York: The Cordon Company.

Horn, R.E. (1982). Structured writing and text design. In D.H. Jonassen (Ed.), *The technology of text: Principles for structuring, designing, and displaying text* (pp. 341–367). Englewood Cliffs, NJ: Educational Technology Publications.

Information power: Guidelines for school library media programs. (1988). Washington, D.C.: American Association of School Librarians and Association for Educational Communications and Technology.

International Board of Standards for Training, Performance, and Instruction, Chicago: IBSTPI.

Instructional Design Competencies: The Standards (1986)

Instructor Competencies: The Standards (Vol. I, 1988; Vol. I, 2nd. Ed.; 1993; Vol. II, 1992).

The Training Manager Competencies: The Standards (1989).

Jacobs, R.L. (1988). A proposed domain of human performance technology: Implications for theory and practice. *Performance Improvement Quarterly, 1*(2), 2–12.

Joint Committee on Standards for Educational Evaluation. (1981). *Standards for evaluations of educational programs, projects, and materials.* New York: McGraw Hill Book Company.

Jonassen, D.H. (1982). *The technology of text: Principles for structuring, designing, and displaying text*. Englewood Cliffs, NJ: Educational Technology Publications.

Jonassen, D.H. (1988). *Instructional designs for micro-computer courseware*. Hillsdale, NJ: Lawrence Erlbaum Associates, Publisher.

Jonassen, D.H. (Ed.). (forthcoming). *Handbook of research on educational communications and technology*. New York: Scholastic Publishing Company.

Joyce, B. and Weil, M. (1972). *Models of teaching*. Englewood Cliffs, NJ: Prentice Hall.

Kaufman, R. (1972). *Educational system planning*. Englewood Cliffs, NJ: Prentice Hall.

Kaufman, R. (1985). Linking training to organizational impact. *Journal of Instructional Development, 8*(2), 23–29.

Kaufman, R. (1986). A Glossary of Planning and Organizational Improvement Terms. In *An Introduction to Performance Technology Volume 1*. (pp. 52–56). Washington, DC: National Society for Performance and Instruction.

Kaufman, R. and English, F. (1979). *Needs Assessment: Concept and Application*. Englewood Cliffs, NJ: Educational Technology Publications

Keeves, J.P. (1989). Knowledge diffusion in education. In M. Eraut (Ed.), *The international encyclopedia of educational technology*. (pp. 582–590). Oxford: Pergamon Press.

Keller, J.M. (1979). Motivation and instructional design: A theoretical perspective. *Journal of Instructional Development, 2*(4), 26–33.

Keller, J.M. (1983). Motivational design of instruction. In C.M. Reigeluth (Ed.), *Instructional-design theories and models: An overview of their current status* (pp. 383–434). Hillsdale, NJ: Lawrence Erlbaum Associates, Publishers.

Keller, J.M. (1987a). Strategies for stimulating the motivation to learn. *Performance and Instruction, 26*(9), 1–7.

Keller, J.M. (1987b). The systematic process of motivational design. *Performance and Instruction. 26*(10), 1–8.

Kember, D., and Murphy, D. (1990). Alternative new directions for instructional design. *Educational Technology, 30*(8), 42–47.

Kemp, J. and Dayton, D. K. (1985). *Planning and producing educational media.* New York: Harper and Row.

Kemp, J. E. and Smellie, D. C. (1989). *Planning, producing and using instructional media* (6th Ed.). NY: Harper Collins.

Kilpatrick, W.H. (1925). *Foundations of method.* New York: Macmillan Press.

Knezek, G.; Rachlin, S.; and Scannell, P. (1988). A taxonomy for educational computing. *Educational Technology, 28*(3), 18–19.

Knirk, F. G. and Gustafson, K.L. (1986). *Instructional technology: A systematic approach to education.* New York: Holt, Rinehart and Winston.

Knezevich, S.J. and Eye, G.G. (Eds.). (1970). *Instructional technology and the school administration.* Washington, D.C.: American Assoication of School Administrators.

Knowlton, D.C. and Tilton, J.W. (1929). *Motion pictures in history teaching.* New Haven, CT: Yale Univeristy Press.

Kozma, R.B. (1991). Learning with media. *Review of Educational Research, 61*(2), 179–211.

Kozma, R. and Bangert-Downs, R. (1987). *Design in context: A conceptual framework for the study of computer software in higher education.* (Grant No. OERI-8-0010). Ann Arbor, MI: University of Michigan (ED28736).

Krathwohl, D.R.; Bloom, B.S.; and Masia, B.B. (1964). *Taxonomy of educational objectives, Handbook II: Affective domain.* New York: David McKay Company.

Kuhn, T. S. (1962). *The structure of scientific disciplines.* Chicago: The University of Chicago Press.

Lajoie, S.P. (1993). Computer environments as cognitive tools for enhancing learning. In S.P. Lajoie and S.J. Derry (Ed.), *Computers as cognitive tools* (pp. 201–288). Hillsdale, NJ: Lawrence Earlbaum Associates, Publishers.

Lazerfield, P., et.al. (1944). *The people's choice.* New York: Duell, Sloan, and Pearce.

Leshin, C.B.; Pollock, J.; and Reigeluth, C.M. (1992). *Instructional design strategies and tactics.* Englewood Cliffs, NJ: Educational Technology Publications.

Lindenmayer, G. (1988). Information technology. In D. Unwin and R. McAleese (Eds.), *The encyclopaedia of educational media communications and technology* (pp. 310–320). New York: Greenwood Press.

Lochte, R. H. (1993). *Interactive television and instruction.* Englewood Cliffs, NJ: Educational Technology Publications.

Lockard, J., Abrams, P. D. and Many, W. A. (1987). *Microcomputers for educators.* Boston: Little Brown.

Lumsdaine, A.A. (1964). Educational technology, programmed learning, and instructional science. In E.R. Hilgard (Ed.), *Theories of learning and instruction.* The sixty-third yearbook of the National Society for the Study of Education, Part I. Chicago: The University of Chicago Press.

Lumsdaine, A.A. and Glaser, R. (1960). *Teaching machines and programmed learning: A source book.* Washington, D.C.: Department of Audio-Visual Instruction, National Education Association.

Mager, R.L. (1962). *Preparing instructional objectives.* Palo Alto, CA: Fearon Publishers.

Margulies, N. and Raia, A.P. (1972). *Organizational development: Values, process, and technology.* New York: McGraw Hill Book Company.

Marriner-Tomey, A. (1989). *Nursing theorists and their work.* St. Louis: C.V. Mosby Company.

Martin, B.L and Briggs, L.J. (1986). *The affective and cognitive domains: Integration for instruction and research.* Englewood Cliffs, NJ: Educational Technology Publications.

Martin, B.L. and Clemente, R. (1990). Instructional systems design and public schools. *Educational Technology Research and Development, 38*(2), 61–76.

Mayer, R.E. (1982). Learning. In H.E. Mitzel (Ed.), *Encyclopedia of educational research* (pp. 1040–1058). New York: The Free Press.

McCombs, B. (1986). The instructional systems development (ISD) model: A review of those factors critical to the successful implementation. *Educational Communications and Technology Journal*, 34(2), 67–81.

McLuhan, M. (1964). *Understanding media: The extensions of man.* New York: McGraw Hill.

Merrill, M.D. (1983). Component display theory. In C.M. Reigeluth (Ed.), *Instructional-design theories and models: An overview of their current status* (pp. 279–333). Hillsdale, NJ: Lawrence Erlbaum Associates, Publishers.

Merrill, M.D; Li, A. and Jones, M.K. (1990). The second generation instructional design research program. *Educational Technology, 31*(5), 45–53.

Merrill, M.D.; Tennyson, R.D. and Posey, L.O. (1992). *Teaching concepts: An instructional design guide* (2nd Ed.). Englewood Cliffs, NJ: Educational Technology Publications.

Miller, R. L.; Syers, J.; Reeve, V. and Kaston, A. (1991). *Multimedia and related technologies: A glossary of terms.* Falls Church, VA: Future Systems, Inc.

Misanchuk, E.R. (1978). Descriptors of evaluations in instructional development: Beyond the formative-summative distinction. *Journal of Instructional Development, 2*(1), 15–19.

Mokyr, J. (1990). *The lever of riches: Technological creativity and economic progress.* New York: Oxford University Press.

Molenda, M. (1993). The domain of utilization. A paper presented at the 1993 Annual Meeting of the Association for Educational Communications and Technology in New Orleans, LA.

Mood, A. (1964). Some problems inherent in the development of a systems approach to instruction. A paper presented at the Conference on New Dimensions for Research in Educational Media Implied by the Systems Approach to Education, Syracuse University.

Morehouse, D.L. (1987). Evaluating interactive television: Methods, findings and issues. Analysis based on evaluation of Minnesota's Technology Demonstration Program. A paper presented at the Annual Conference on Teaching at a Distance. (ERIC Document Reproduction Service No. ED 182 465).

Morgan, R.M. (1987). Planning for instructional systems. In R.M. Gagné (Ed.), *Instructional technology: Foundations* (pp. 379–396). Hillsdale, NJ: Lawwrence Erlbaum Associates.

Morris, B.J. et al. (Eds.). (1992). *Administering the school library media center*. New Providence, NJ: Bowker.

Morris, L. L. (Ed.). (1978). *Program evaluation kit*. Beverly Hills, CA: Sage Publications. A series developed by the Center for the Study of Evaluation (CES), University of California at Los Angeles.

Performance & Instruction, 23(1). February, 1984. Theme Issue on Professional Certification.

Petroski, H. (1992). *To engineer is human*. New York: Vintage Books.

Pettersson, R. (1993). *Visuals for information: Research and practice* (2nd Ed.). Englewood Cliffs, NJ: Educational Technology Publications.

Polson, M.C. (1993). Cognitive theory as a basis for instructional design. In J.M. Spector, M.C. Polson, and D.J. Muraida (Eds.), *Automating instructional design* (pp. 5–22). Englewood Cliffs, NJ: Educational Technology Publications.

Popham, W. J. (1973). *Criterion-referenced instruction*. Palo Alto, CA: Fearon Publishers.

Priestley, M. (1982) *Performance assessment in education and training: Alternative techniques*. Englewood Cliffs NJ: Educational Technology Publications.

Prostano, E.T. and Prostano, J.S. (1987). *The school library media center* (4th Ed.): Englewood,CO: Libraries Unlimited.

Reeves, T.C. (1992). Evaluating interactive media. *Educational Technology, 32*(5), 47–53.

Reigeluth, C.M. (Ed.). (1983). *Instructional-design theories and models: An overview of their current status*. Hillsdale, NJ: Lawrence Erlbaum Associates.

Reigeluth, C.M. (1983a). Instructional design: What is it and why is it? In C.M. Reigeluth (Ed.), *Instructional-design theories and models: An overview of their current status* (pp. 3–36). Hillsdale, NJ: Lawrence Erlbaum Associates.

Reigeluth, C.M. (Ed.). (1987). *Instructional theories in action*. Hillsdale, NJ: Lawrence Erlbaum Associates.

Reigeluth, C.M. and Curtis, R.V. (1987). Learning situations and instructional models. In R.M. Gagné (Ed.), *Instructional technology: Foundations* (pp. 175–206). Hillsdale, NJ: Lawrence Erlbaum Associates.

Reiser, R. and Gagné, R.M. (1982). *The selection of media for instruction*. Englewood Cliffs, NJ: Educational Technology Publications.

Reynolds, A. and Anderson, R.H. (1991). *Selecting and developing media for instruction* (3rd Ed.). New York: Van Nostrand Rinehold.

Richey, R.C. (1986). *The theoretical and conceptual bases of instructional design*. London: Kogan Page.

Richey, R.C. (1992). *Designing instruction for the adult learner: Systemic training theory and practice*. London: Kogan Page.

Richey, R.C. (1993a). Instructional design theory and a changing field. *Educational Technology, 33*(2), 16–21.

Richey, R.C. (1993b). The knowledge base of instructional design. A paper presented at the 1993 Annual Meeting of the Association for Educational Communications and Technology in New Orleans, LA.

Richey, R.C. and Sikorski, J. (1993). Instructional design can make a difference in staff development. *Journal of Staff Development, 14*(2), 44–47.

Rogers, E.M. (1962). *Diffusion of innovations*. New York: The Free Press.

Rogers, E.M. (1983). *Diffusion of innovations* (3rd Ed.). New York: The Free Press.

Rogers, E.M. and Shoemaker, F.F. (1971). *Communication of innovation: A cross-cultural approach* (2nd Ed.). New York: Free Press.

Roller, D.H. (Ed.). (1971). *Perspectives in the history of science and technology*. Norman, OK: University of Oklahoma Press.

Romiszowski, A. (1988). *The selection and use of instructional media* (2nd. Ed.). London: Kogan Page, Ltd.

Romiszowski, A. (1981). *Designing instructional systems: Decision making in courseplanning and curriculum design*. London: Kogan Page, Ltd.

Rosenberg, K. C. and Elsbree, J. J. (1989). *Dictionary of library and educational technology*. Englewood, CO: Libraries Unlimited.

Ross, S.M. and Morrison, G.R. (1989). In search of a happy medium in instructional technology research: Issues concerning external validity, media replications, and learner control. *Educational Technology Research and Development, 37*(1), 19–33.

Rossett, A. (1987). *Training needs assessment*. Englewood Cliffs, NJ: Educational Technology Publications.

Rothwell, W.J. and Kazanas, H.C. (1992). *Mastering the instructional design process: A systematic approach*. San Francisco: Jossey-Bass.

Rountree, D. (1979). Conceptions of educational technology. A paper presented at the 1979 Conference of European Educational Technology (pp. 1–12).

Saettler, P. (1968). *A history of instructional technology.* New York: McGraw-Hill Book Company.

Saettler, P. (1990). *The evolution of American educational technology.* Englewood, CO: Libraries Unlimited.

Salomon, G. (1992). New information technologies in education. In M.C. Alkin (Ed.), *Encyclopedia of educational research* (6th Ed.) (pp. 892–903). New York: Macmillan Publishing Company.

Scheffler, I. (1960). *The language of education.* Springfield, IL: Charles C. Thomas Publisher.

Schramm, W.L. (1954). How communication works. In W. Schramm and D.F. Roberts (Eds.), *The process and effects of mass communication* (pp. 3–26). Urbana, IL: University of Illinois Press.

Schwartz, F.D. (1992). Notes from the field: Shop talk. *American Heritage of Invention and Technology, 7,* 6–7.

Schwier, R. (1987). *Interactive video.* Englewood Cliffs, NJ: Educational Technology Publications.

Schwier, R. A. and Misanchuk, E. R. (1993). *Interactive multimedia instruction.* Englewood Cliffs, NJ: Educational Technology Publications.

Scriven, M. (1967). *The methodology of evaluation.* AERA Monograph Series on Curriculum Evaluation, No. 1. Chicago: Rand McNally.

Scriven, M. (1980). *Evaluation thesaurus* (2nd Ed.). Inverness, CA: Edgepress.

Seels, B. (1989). The instructional design movement in educational technology. *Educational Technology, 29*(5), 11–15.

Seels, B. (1993). The knowledge base of the evaluation domain. (ERIC Document Reproduction Service No. ED 355 919).

Seels, B. (Ed.). (1993a). Instructional design fundamentals: A review and reconsideration. Introduction to a special issue. *Educational Technology, 33*(2), 7–8.

Seels, B. (1993b). The view looking back: Curriculum theory and instructional technology programs. *Educational Technology, 33*(2), 21–27.

Seels, B. (1993c). The knowledge base of evaluation. A paper presented at the 1993 Annual Meeting of the Association for Educational Communications and Technology at New Orleans, LA.

Seels, B. (1993d). Visual literacy: The definition problem. In D.M. Moore and F. Dwyer (Eds.), *Visual literacy: A spectrum of visual learning* (pp. 97–112). Englewood Cliffs, NJ: Educational Technology Publications.

Seels, B. and Glasgow, Z. (1991). Survey of instructional design needs and competencies. In M.R. Simonson and C. Hargrave (Eds.), *Proceedings of selected research presentations at the 1991 annual convention of the Association for Educational Communications and Technology* (pp. 995–1004). (ERIC Document Reproduction Service No. ED 334 969).

Seels, B. and Glasgow, Z. (1990). *Exercises in instructional design.* Columbus, OH: Merrill Publishers.

Shannon, C. and Weaver, W. (1949). *The mathematical theory of communication.* Urbana: University of Illinois Press.

Shelly, G. B. and Cashman, T. J. (1980). *Introduction to computers and data processing.* Brea, CA: Anaheim Publishing.

Shrock, S. A. and Coscarelli, W. C. C. (1989). *Criterion-referenced test development.* Reading, MA: Addison-Wesley.

Shulman, L. S. (1986). Paradigms and research programs in the study of teaching: A comtemporary perspective. In M. C. Wittrock (Ed.), *Handbook of research on teaching* (pp. 3–36). New York: Macmillan Publishing Company.

Silber, K. (1970). What field are we in, anyhow? *Audiovisual Instruction, 15*(5), 21–24.

Silber, K. (Ed.). (1979). *Educational technology: A glossary of terms.* Washington, D.C.: Association for Educational Communications and Technology.

Simon, H.A. (1969). *The sciences of the artificial.* Cambridge, MA: MIT Press.

Simonson, M. (1993). The knowledge base of the development domain. A paper presented at the 1993 Annual Meeting of the Association for Educational Communications and Technology at New Orleans, LA.

Simonson, M. R. and Volker, R. P. (1984). *Media planning and production.* Columbus, OH: Charles E. Merrill.

Skinner, B.F. (1954). The science of learning and the art of teaching. *Harvard Educational Review, 24,* 86–97.

Skinner, B.F. (1968). *The technology of teaching.* New York: Meredith Corporation.

Smith, P.L. and Ragan, T.J. (1993). Designing instructional feedback for different learning outcomes. In J.V. Dempsey and G.C. Sales (Eds.), *Interactive instruction and feedback* (pp. 75–103). Englewood Cliffs, NJ: Educational Technology Publications.

Smith, P.L. and Ragan, T.J. (1993a). *Instructional design.* New York: Macmillan Publishing Company.

Sokal, R. (1974). Classification: Purposes, principles, progress, prospect. *Science,* 185.

Sonnier, I. L. (1989). *Affective education: Methods and techniques.* Englewood Cliffs, NJ: Educational Technology Publications.

Spencer, K. (1988). *The psychology of educational technology and instructional media.* London: Routledge

Striebel, M.J. (1991). A critical analysis of the use of computers in education. In D. Hlynka and J.C. Belland (Eds.), *Paradigms regained: The uses of illuminative, semiotic and post-modern criticism as modes of inquiry in educational technology* (pp. 283–334). Englewood Cliffs, NJ: Educational Technology Publications.

Stufflebeam, D.L. (1969). Evaluation as enlightenment for decision making. In W.A. Beatty (Ed.), *Improving educational assessment and an inventory of measures of affective behavior.* Washington, D.C.: Association for Supervision and Curriculum Development.

Stufflebeam, D.L. (1983). The CIPP Model for Program Evaluation. In G.F. Madaus, M. Scriven, and Stufflebeam, D.L. (Eds.), *Evaluation models: Viewpoints on educational and human services evaluation.* (pp. 117–141). Boston: Kluwer-Nijhoff.

Task Force on ID Certification. (1981). Competencies for the instructional/training development professional. *Journal of Instructional Development, 5*(1), 14–15.

Tennyson, R. D. (1990). Instructional design theory: Advancements from cognitive science and instructional technology. In M.R. Simonson and C. Hargrave (Eds.), *Proceedings of selected research paper presentations at the 1990 annual convention of the Association for Educational Communications and Technology* (pp. 609–630). (ERIC Document Reproduction Service No. ED 323 951).

Tessmer, M. (1990). Environmental analysis: A neglected stage of instructional design. *Educational Technology Research and Development, 38*(1), 55–64.

Tessmer. M. (1993). *Planning and conducting formative evaluation: Improving the quality of education and training.* London: Kogan Page.

Tessmer, M. and Harris, D. (1992). *Analysing the instructional setting: Environmental analysis.* London: Kogan Page.

Thompson, A.D.; Simonson, M.R.; and Hargrave, C.P. (1992). *Educational technology: A review of the research.* Washington, D.C.: Association for Educational Communications and Technology.

Ticton, G. (1971). *To improve learning.* A report by the Commission on Instructional Technology. New York: Bowker.

Tobias, S. (1987). Learner characteristics. In R. M. Gagné (Ed.), *Instructional technology: Foundations.* (pp. 207–231). Hillsdale, NJ: Lawrence Erlbaum Associates.

Tovar, M. (1988). Visual literacy. In D. Unwin and R. McAleese (Eds.), *The encyclopaedia of educational media communications and technology* (2nd. ed.) (pp. 550–553). New York: Greenwood Press.

Toynbee, A.J. (1957). *A study of history.* New York: Oxford University Press.

Training (The Magazine of Human Resources Development). Industry Report: An Overview of Employee Training in America, (An annual report in the October issue.).

Tyler, R.W. (1950). *Basic principles of curriculum and instruction: Syllabus for Education 305*. Chicago: University of Chicago Press.

UNESCO. (1984). *Glossary of educational technology terms*. NY: French and European Publications. Available in French and English.

Unwin, D. and McAleese, R. (Eds.). (1988). *The encyclopaedia of educational media communications and technology* (2nd Ed.). NY: Greenwood Press.

Vanderschmidt, H. and Segall, A. (1985). An instructional system as change agent. *Journal of Instructional Development, 8*(1), 18–21).

Venezky, R. and Osin, L. (1991). *The intelligent design of computer-assisted instruction*. NY: Longman.

Vlcek, C.W. and Wiman, R.V. (1989). *Managing media services: Theory and practice*. Englewood, CO: Libraries Unlimited.

Wager, W.W. (1993). Instructional systems fundamentals: Pressures to change. *Educational Technology, 33*(2), 8–12.

Wager, W.W.; Applefield, J.M.; Earle, R.S.; and Dempsey, J.W. (1990). *Principles of instructional design*. Chicago: Holt, Rinehart, and Winston.

Walker, W. G. (1973). *Glossary of educational terms: Usage in five English-Speaking countries*. St. Lucia, Queensland: University of Queensland Press.

Wallington, C.J.; Hyer, A.L.; Bernotavicz, F.D.; Hale, P.; and Silber, K. (1970). *Jobs in instructional media*. Washington, D.C.: AECT.

Welliver, P. (1989). The AECT code of professional ethics: A guide to professional conduct in the field. *Tech Trends, 34*(5), 52–53.

Westley, B.H. and MacLean, M.S. (1957). A conceptual model for communication research. *Journalism Quarterly, 34*, 31–38.

Wileman, R.E. (1993). *Visual communicating*. Englewood Cliffs, NJ: Educational Technology Publications.

Willis, B. (1993). *Distance education: A practical guide*. Englewood Cliffs, NJ: Educational Technology Publications.

Willows, D.M. and Houghton, H.A. (1987). *The psychology of illustration, volume 1: Basic research*. New York: Springer-Verlag.

Wiman, R.V. and Meierhenry, W.C. (1969). *Educational media: Theory into practice*. Columbus, OH: Charles E. Merrill Publishing Company.

Winn, W. (1989). Toward a rationale and theoretical basis for educational technology. *Educational Technology Research and Development, 37*(1), 35–46.

Winn, W. (1993). Instructional design and situated learning: Paradox or partnership? *Educational Technology, 33*(3), 16–21.

Wolfe, P.; Wetzel, M.; Harris, G.; Mazour, T. and Riplinger, J. (1991). *Job task analysis: Guide to good practice*. Englewood Cliffs, NJ: Educational Technology Publications.

Wood, B.D. and Freeman, F.N. (1929). *Motion pictures in the classroom*. Boston: Houghton Mifflin.

Worthen, B.R. and Sanders, J.R. (1973). *Educational evaluation: Theory and practice*. Worthington, OH: Charles A. Jones.

Worthen, B.R. and Sanders, J.R. (1987). *Educational evaluation: Alternative approaches and practical guidelines*. New York: Longman.

INDEX

Author Index

Subject Index